BOURGEOIS, SANS-CULOTTES, AND OTHER FRENCHMEN

ESSAYS ON THE FRENCH REVOLUTION IN HONOR OF JOHN HALL STEWART

EDITED BY
MORRIS SLAVIN AND AGNES M. SMITH

Few events are as complex as a social revolution—as the disputes among historians over the nature of the French Revolution attest. Was it Atlantic or national, bourgeois or *sans-culotte*, a product of poverty or prosperity, one revolution or several? The essays in this volume, in honour of an eminent student of the Revolution, demonstrate the complexity once again. Stanley Idzerda and Ruth Strong Hudson consider the cases of two individuals influential in the Revolution, Lafayette and Gérard, while James Harkins investigates the intellectual origins of Babouvism. Themistocles Rodis asks whether morals declined during the Revolution, and Morris Slavin reassesses the effect on the Revolution of the struggle in section Roi de Sicile between monarchists and republicans. Agnes Smith and James Friguglietti examine the assessment of the Revolution by a contemporary observer (Toulongeon) and a twentieth-century historian (Mathiez).

Morris Slavin, Professor of History at Youngstown State University, Ohio, holds the Ph.D. degree from Western Reserve University. His publications have appeared in Annales historiques de la révolution française, *as well as other journals, and he has recently completed a study of Section Droits de l'Homme during the French Revolution.*

Agnes Monroe Smith, Professor of History at Youngstown State University, Ohio, holds the Ph.D. degree from Western Reserve University. Her current research is on the spread of "Mormonism" in England in the nineteenth century.

JOHN HALL STEWART

BOURGEOIS, SANS-CULOTTES, AND OTHER FRENCHMEN

ESSAYS ON THE FRENCH REVOLUTION IN HONOR OF JOHN HALL STEWART

EDITED BY
MORRIS SLAVIN AND AGNES M. SMITH

Wilfrid Laurier University Press

944.04
B772

Canadian Cataloguing in Publication Data

Main entry under title:
Bourgeois, sans-culottes, and other Frenchmen

Includes index.
ISBN 0-88920-097-1

1. France — History — Revolution, 1789-1799 —
Addresses, essays, lectures.   2. Stewart, John
Hall, 1904-   I. Stewart, John Hall, 1904-
II. Slavin, Morris, 1913-   III. Smith, Agnes M.
(Agnes Monroe), 1920-

DC148.B68   944.04   C81-094378-6

Copyright © 1981
WILFRID LAURIER UNIVERSITY PRESS
Waterloo, Ontario, Canada   N2L 3C5

81 82 83 84 4 3 2 1

83-3315

Contents

Contents

Notes on the Contributors

James Friguglietti studied with John Hall Stewart at Western Reserve University before earning his doctoral degree at Harvard in 1966. He is author of *The Shaping of Modern France* (1969), *Bibliographie de Georges Lefebvre* (1972) and *Albert Mathiez, Historien révolutionnaire (1874-1932)* (1974), and has translated (with John Hall Stewart) the second volume of Georges Lefebvre's *La Revolution française*.

James R. Harkins received his Ph.D. at Western Reserve University in 1965 and is Associate Professor of History at Wilfrid Laurier University. He has presented papers for the Duquesne History Forum and the Western Society for French History.

Ruth Strong Hudson studied at the Sorbonne, Vassar College, and the University of Strasbourg and received her Ph.D. at Western Reserve University in 1947. She is co-author of *The First Hundred Years: The History of Hathaway Brown School* and is completing a biography of Conrad-Alexandre Gérard.

Stanley J. Idzerda received his doctorate from Western Reserve University in 1951. As Editor-in-Chief of the Lafayette Papers at Cornell University, he has published *Lafayette in the Age of the American Revolution* (1977, 1979). He is Professor of History at the College of St. Benedict.

Themistocles Rodis received his Ph.D. from Western Reserve University in 1968 and has been Professor of History at Baldwin-Wallace College since 1971 and Chairman of the Division of Humanities since 1976. His publications include a number of articles in *The World Book Encyclopedia*, and he is currently completing an introductory text in European history.

Agnes Monroe Smith received her doctorate from Western Reserve University in 1966. She is Professor of History at Youngstown State University and has presented papers at the Ohio Academy of History and the Duquesne History Forum. Her current research is on the spread of "Mormonism" in England in the nineteenth century.

Morris Slavin received his Ph.D. from Western Reserve University in 1961 and is Professor of History at Youngstown State University. His publications have appeared in *Annales historiques de la Révolution française* and in various American historical journals. He has presented papers at the XIVth International Congress of the Historical Sciences and in professional historical gatherings in the U.S.A. and abroad. Recently he has completed a study of Section Droits-de-l'Homme during the French Revolution.

Acknowledgements

It is a pleasure to acknowledge the debt we owe to friends and participants, especially Samuel Miller of the Forest City Products of Cleveland. The Graduate Research Council of Youngstown State University has assisted in various ways, and Mrs. Christine Kelley has labored long and faithfully to type the manuscript.

Introduction

Few acts of man as political animal are as complex as a social revolution. The dispute among historians over the nature of the French Revolution attests to the complexity of that event. Was it Atlantic or national, bourgeois or *sans-culotte*, a product of poverty or of prosperity, one revolution or several? It is certain that these questions will not be resolved before France celebrates the bicentennial of the Revolution in 1989, and doubtful if they will approach resolution at the tricentennial.

The contributions that follow give further proof of this complexity. Two themes alone bind the contributors: the French Revolution as an historical event, and the subtle influence of John Hall Stewart who stimulated the contributors' interest in eighteenth-century France. The varieties of the French Revolution may be seen in the variety of subjects discussed—from the biographical sketch of Albert Mathiez to the intellectual roots of Babeuf's political program, from a *cahier* of Alsace to the observations of a contemporaneous historian, François-Emmanuel Toulongeon.

Although the subjects examined differ, the approach to the Revolution by the contributors is a humanistic one. It is the revolutionary who remains the measure of the Revolution. For better or for worse no contributor has adopted a statistical or a purely demographic approach, nor is there a monolithic point of view either in terms of philosophy or of politics. How pro-Jacobin are the views of the writers? It would be difficult to say. That there are "Robespierrists" among them is probable, but these are balanced, undoubtedly, by "anti-Robespierrists." What interests the essayists, above all, is the reaction of human beings to the Revolution—either as participants in the event, or as historians of it.

Stanley J. Idzerda questions the thesis of the late Louis Gottschalk who argued that Lafayette was no revolutionary even though he had embraced a revolutionary cause in the struggle between America and England. Gottschalk asserted that it was Lafayette's feelings of frustration and inferiority to the courtiers and relatives around him that impelled him to join the American rebels. Idzerda is convinced, however, that Lafayette's commitment to the American Revolution was genuine. He is aware, of course, how difficult it is for historians, no less than for contemporaries, to agree on the term "revolutionary." The

so-called "patriots" of the French Revolution indignantly denied that
there was anything revolutionary about Lafayette, while the Austrians
and Prussians who imprisoned him for five years looked upon the same
man as a dangerous incendiary. To resolve this contradiction Idzerda
offers a definition of the term "revolutionary" in light of which he
judges Lafayette's conduct.

The "Germanic liberties" of Alsace on the eve of the Revolution
are presented by Ruth Hudson, as she describes the historic differences that still separated that province from the rest of France. Especially instructive is the role of the last royal *préteur*, Conrad-Alexandre
Gérard, an ardent defender of his country and an active promoter of
its interests. His brochure, *The Proposed Instructions . . .* , showed
thorough knowledge of administrative and political affairs and became
the basis for the grievances which the *cahier* of Alsace embodied.

Did morals decline during the Revolution, and, if so, how did the
weakening of traditional rules of conduct manifest itself? Or, did
another set of principles replace former standards of behavior?
Themistocles Rodis reminds us that those historians who condemn the
Revolution tend to believe that morals declined. A few, like Mathiez,
although strong supporters of the Revolution, agree with its critics in
this respect. One difficulty that will become evident to readers of this
essay is the problem of erecting a measurable guide by which to judge a
decline in morals. Another, more obvious, is the impossibility of agree-
ing on just what constitutes an improvement of morality. If repression
of sexual desire is lessened and a freer and a more egalitarian relationship develops between the sexes, is this a good or an evil in terms of
morality? The subject being both vast and complex, Rodis limits his
discussion to the problem of marriage and divorce.

Although the role of leading revolutionaries in the overthrow of
the King is well known and the general events of August 9-10, 1792
have been presented by Mortimer-Ternaux, Mellié, Braesch, and
others, the actual developments in a section have seldom been discussed. Morris Slavin attempts to fill this gap by analyzing the struggle
in section Roi-de-Sicile, the future Droits-de-l'Homme, between the
moderates devoted to maintaining a constitutional monarchy, and the
republicans led by the well-known *Enragé*, Jean Varlet. In the course of
his paper he questions the characterization by Fritz Braesch that section Roi-de-Sicile was "moderately conservative" on the eve of the
overthrow of the King.

What is the relationship between objective factors of history and of
human consciousness? Even if we agree that "being determines consciousness" it is the origin, development, and transformation of the
latter into social action that must be examined in itself. An objective,
revolutionary situation can never be transformed into a revolution
without the conscious, human factor of will; hence the importance of

the revolutionary—a Sam Adams, a Robespierre, a Lenin. The problem for historians, is to find the link between objective factors like
hunger, defeat in war, or a raging inflation and the revolutionary idea
as grasped by individuals and their effort to put it into practice. This is
the problem of Babouvism, writes James Harkins. It is not so much
what Rousseau wrote that will unlock the intellectual development of
Babeuf, but rather, what Babeuf *thought* Rousseau wrote that is the key
to his own Rousseauism, Harkins argues. What Babeuf found in the
writings of Rousseau and how he transformed the latter's ideas to serve
his own needs is the theme of Harkins' essay.

Although it is difficult to be objective about contemporary events,
events in which a historian is caught up like any other individual, Agnes
Smith presents one who, if not unbiased, gave a hearing to all partisans
of revolutionary France. Unlike so many of his contemporaries
François-Emmanuel Toulongeon grasped the inevitability of change
in history and utilized the documents that were available to him to
emphasize the flux and flow of the revolutionary waves. Though a
nobleman by birth and a military officer by profession, he took a
surprisingly broad view of the changes France was experiencing. Even
after being forced into emigration he never doubted that the Revolution was caused by "the maturation of things," a sentiment worthy of a
philosopher, writes the author.

Just how present-mindedness affects even the most meticulous of
scholars is reflected in the life and writings of Albert Mathiez. The
corruption of the Third Republic under which he grew up confirmed
the great historian in his socialism which was "republican, anti-clerical,
and idealistic," writes James Friguglietti. The contradiction between
the shabby political reality of his day, and the Jacobin ideal which
Mathiez shared, led him to view Danton with suspicion and to embrace
Robespierre instead. Psychologically unable to separate the past from
the present, Mathiez attacked Alphonse Aulard, his former teacher
and defender of Danton, as if he were the Incorruptible himself
prosecuting the *pourris*, the corrupt deputies, before the bar of public
opinion. This interesting theme is presented in a brief sketch by the
author whose biography of Mathiez was published recently in France.

If no definitive conclusion can be gathered from these explora-
tions of aspects of the French Revolution, this, in itself, is a tribute to
the teacher who inspired them. Whatever point of view John Hall
Stewart held on this seminal event of the eighteenth century, he never
sought to impose it on his graduate students. These different points of
view, in addition to the variety of subjects considered, are proof of
Professor Stewart's own approach to history in general and to the
history of the French Revolution in particular.

Like Thomas Mann's Settembrini, John Hall Stewart is a liberal in
the traditional sense—broad, humanistic, tolerant. Nothing is more

alien to his character than the Jacobin or royalist zealot, the revolution-ary fanatic, the *enragé*. This tolerance and humanitarianism enables him to understand the different types of historical personalities from Right to Left without embracing, necessarily, their partisan points of view. Perhaps this is why he turned from the Revolution as politics and became attracted to it as a cultural expression. Always concerned with literature as a prime form of culture, he turned a portion of his creative energies into editing French documents and translating Lefebvre's great synthesis.

Born April 20, 1904 near Springfield, Ontario, not far from London (Canada), a descendent of English and Scottish-Irish immi-grants, he absorbed early in life, values shared by so many immigrant families in the New World—hard work and education. This commit-ment to study was strengthened as the family sacrificed its own comfort to give advantages to young John. Having taken his B.A. in 1927 from the University of Toronto, he earned his advanced degrees at Cornell University with a dissertation on Rabaut St. Etienne. His major work in the latter institution was with Carl Becker and Preserved Smith, which may account for the infectious enthusiasm that he brought to the study of intellectual history.

Upon graduating from Cornell in 1930 he received an appoint-ment at Western Reserve University where he moved up through the ranks to become Professor of History in 1951. From 1954 until his retirement in 1969 he was Henry E. Bourne Professor of History at Western Reserve University (from 1967 to 1969 Case Western Reserve University). His publications in the field of the French Revolution— most notably, *A Guide to Materials in Cleveland* and *A Documentary Survey of the French Revolution*—have brought renown both to him and to the University he served.

He is also the author of *The Restoration Era in France, 1814-1830* in the Anvil Series edited by Louis L. Snyder and of *The French Revolution: Some Trends in Historical Writing, 1945-1965* published by the American Historical Association Service Center for Teachers of History. In col-laboration with James Friguglietti he translated the second part of Georges Lefebvre's *La Révolution française*. Additional articles, pam-phlets, book reviews, and portions of books edited by others are listed in the appendix.

A member of Phi Beta Kappa and numerous other organizations, both honorary and professional, he has been active in academic pur-suits on both the state and the national level. In 1958 he served as President of the Society for French Historical Studies, and in 1961 he was designated by the Government of France as *Officier dans l'ordre des palmes académiques*.

The variety of subjects upon which he has been asked to review books is a tribute to his wide competence. The range of his concerns, which also took him into Irish studies and Canadian history, is evidenced in many of his publications. In articles on the French Revolution as related to Ireland, he combines two of his favorite research topics. In 1961 two men were elected Fellows of the Royal Society of Antiquaries of Ireland: Eamon de Valera and John Hall Stewart.

Nor have the activities and the honors ceased with his retirement. At the invitation of his former students he was persuaded to moderate sessions at the Ohio Academy of History in 1974 and at the Duquesne History Forum in 1976 and 1978. He participated in the program of the Consortium on Revolutionary Europe in 1979. In April, 1976 he received the Ohio Academy of History Award for Distinguished Service to the Historical Profession.

The seven essays presented in Professor Stewart's honor are our acknowledgement of his influence on our own academic development. His five former doctoral candidates, Stanley J. Idzerda, Morris Slavin, James B. Harkins, Agnes Smith, and Themistocles C. Rodis, as well as his one-time graduate students, Ruth S. Hudson and James Frigugli-etti, feel indebted to the influence of his scholarship and personality and are represented in the essays that follow. We dedicate this book as a tribute to him and present it as a token of our regard.

Morris Slavin and Agnes M. Smith, Editors

When and Why Lafayette Became a Revolutionary

STANLEY J. IDZERDA

Marquis de Lafayette was consistently identified with revolutions and incitement to revolution between 1776 and 1834. He never denied the charge; rather, he encouraged it and seemed to glory in the identification. Thus it would appear to be a relatively simple matter to find out when, why, and how Lafayette became a revolutionary. After making a straightforward inquiry into the ideas, habits, motives, and attitudes which gave his character a revolutionary cast or predisposition, all that remains is to discover the date upon which he became personally involved in a revolution.

But there are several reasons why the question may not submit to such a straightforward inquiry. We are in a time when the name "revolution" is attached to almost any short- or long-run change, and the name "revolutionary" is given to its leaders. Common sense understanding of the terms is deceptive, and we lack adequate, agreed-upon definitions of these words in the scholarly community. Serious critical studies of the concept and the act of "revolution" sometimes seem to verge on despair as they seek light in the surrounding epistemological gloom. The editor of a recent trio of intensive analyses of revolutions commented that "the very concept of revolution remains elusive"; and Peter Zagorin, author of one of the essays, notes that on the essential question of what is to be understood by "revolution," "one finds a striking absence of clarity, consistency or agreement."[1] In his 1972 study of definitions and explanations of revolutions, Isaac Kramnick concluded that the scholarly accounts of revolutions and revolutionaries are a "confused, complicated and untidy set of observations"; his critique does not differ in its overall result from the acid bath which Barbara Salert offers the four leading theoretical constructs in her 1976 volume, *Revolutions and Revolutionaries*.[2]

For the purposes of this paper the muddle is made even muddier by the fact that it has long been the habit of writers on revolution to

---

1 *Comparative Studies in Society and History*, 18 (1976), 149, 152.
2 Isaac Kramnick, "Reflections on Revolution: Definition and Explanation in Recent Scholarship," *History and Theory*, 11 (1972), 26; Barbara Salert, *Revolution and Revolutionaries: Four Theories* (New York, 1976).

concentrate upon the French and the Russian Revolutions as the only "real," "complete," or "comprehensive" revolutions; they seem to have genuine difficulty finding a place for the American Revolution in their typological framework. In truth, most modern studies mention the American Revolution in passing as a special case or as an exception. Most often, it is simply ignored. Since Lafayette served in the American army during the American Revolution, we have to take into account the peculiar categorical problem that "revolution" presents to most scholars, even while we may be given pause to discover that Lafayette himself referred to the American war for independence as both a revolution and a civil war during his first six months on this continent.[3]

Lafayette also served in a number of French civil and military posts during the French Revolution. Upon being impeached in 1792, he emigrated, was captured by the Austrians, and spent five years in Austrian and Prussian prisons. How, and to what extent, is one defined as, or does one qualify as a "revolutionary" if one has not persisted to the "end" of the revolution? A corollary: does a person still qualify as a revolutionary if those who have successfully co-opted the "patriot" title consider him a counter-revolutionary? A reading of the extended comments of Lafayette's accusers during the first half of 1792 could suggest that Lafayette had never been a revolutionary at any time during the French Revolution.

In this welter of debate, the student of the subject is obliged to offer a working definition of terms. For the purposes of this essay, I shall define a *revolution* as "an organized attempt to bring about a relatively rapid, major change in government structure and policy, accompanied by violence or the threat of violence." A *revolutionary* I shall define as "the self-conscious, wilful participant in a revolution who has good cause to understand that his or her motives and goals for the revolution are shared by most other participants in it." In the definition of "revolution" I intend to exclude the coup d'état, palace revolt, or other forms of violent change which simply change the hands on the reins of power, or which have no program for fundamental change in government structure and policy. In the definition of "revolutionary," I intend to exclude the participant whose motives may be adventure or the conscious or unconscious need to vent frustrations and aggressions based upon conditions peculiar to his or her personal history. This is not to say that a palace revolt or coup is not sometimes called a revolution, or that there are not many participants in revolutions out of motives of ennui or unfocused aggression; it is to say that these acts or motives will not qualify under these definitions. The definitions are not without flaw, but they are defensible and they will set the boundaries of my discussion of Lafayette as a revolutionary.

3 "Civil War" in a letter to Adrienne, October 29, 1777; "Revolution" in letter to Duc d'Ayen, December 16, 1777, Cornell University: *Dean Collection*.

The second set of reasons why a straightforward inquiry into the beginnings of Lafayette's presumed career as a revolutionary is not possible is that Louis Gottschalk's intensive, six-volume, 2,400-page chronicle of Lafayette's life up through the early years of the French Revolution has pre-empted the field. In none of these six volumes does Gottschalk indicate that Lafayette was ever a revolutionary. Gottschalk's definition of a revolution: "a popular movement whereby a significant change in the structure of a nation or a society is affected," probably covers the case of the American Revolution.[4] Yet ever since the appearance of his *Lafayette Comes to America* forty years ago, scholars and reference books have cited Gottschalk's findings, namely, that Lafayette's claim that he came to America in 1777 because he shared the goals of the Americans for liberty and independence is nothing more than a "myth" and a "legend" perpetrated and fostered by Lafayette himself.[5] Thus any attempt to show that Lafayette was a revolutionary in America will have to contend with accepted scholarly opinion; it will also have to meet Gottschalk's arguments on their own terms as well as within the terms of the definitions offered above. The rest of this paper will then offer (1) a bald summary of Lafayette's voyage to America in that year; (2) a discussion of the milieu from which Lafayette came which supports a contention that Lafayette was a revolutionary when he joined the American army; and (3) Lafayette's own testimony in the years 1776 and 1777 concerning his state of mind and his motivations for casting his lot with the American cause.

II

A chronicle of the agreed upon details of Lafayette's life up to June, 1777, is easily related.[6] He was born on September 6, 1757, at Chavaniac in Auvergne. His family were members of the *noblesse d'epée* who had fought and died for their king and country since the Crusades. Lafayette's father was killed at the battle of Minden when Lafayette was two years old; his mother thereafter lived with her relatives in Paris, about 500 kilometers from Chavaniac, for most of the year. The boy stayed behind at Chavaniac, and his upbringing remained in the hands of his grandmother and his aunts until he was eleven years old. In that year (1768) he was brought to Paris by his mother and lived with her and her family at the Palais du Luxembourg. In the same year he was enrolled in the Collège du Plessis at about the same time that Robespierre entered the nearby Collège Louis le Grand. Lafayette remained at the College for four years under the aegis of a

4 L. Gottschalk, "Causes of Revolution," *American Journal of Sociology*, 50 (1944), 4.
5 L. Gottschalk, *Lafayette Comes to America* (Chicago, 1935).
6 They are most readily found in *Lafayette Comes to America*, or in E. Charavay, *Le Général La Fayette* (Paris, 1898).

classical curriculum, with heavy doses from the poets and philosophers of the late Roman Republic, laced with the moralizing histories of Rome by Rollin and the exemplary biographies of Plutarch. He was a good student and won a prize for Latin composition.

The Lafayette family at Chavaniac had been endowed with moderate means and the only scion of the line was raised in a style in keeping with those means. Then, within a few weeks during Lafayette's thirteenth year, there was a double reversal of fortune: the deaths of his mother and his maternal grandfather left him an orphan but also left him wealthy. Suddenly he commanded an income of at least 120,000 livres per year. Since the accident of birth had provided the young man with sufficient quarterings and the accidents of death provided him with a handsome income, the powerful and influential Noailles family decided that Lafayette would be an eligible spouse; he was married to their daughter Adrienne in April, 1774, when Lafayette was 16 and she was 14. Their first child was born in 1775 and the second in 1777. The marriage was a stable one and remained so until the death of Adrienne in 1807.

The Noailles influence enabled Lafayette to enter the army in a notable regiment in 1773; in 1774 he was a captain, with the notation, "*fort joli sujet*" in his dossier.[7] Most of his service was relatively dull duty in the garrison at Metz; in June, 1776, the efforts of the Minister of War, St. Germain, to restructure the army meant that many young officers were to be placed in an inactive reserve status; Lafayette was one of them.

The struggles of the American colonies with Britain had been the subject of excited discussion in France since at least the summer of 1775; indeed, Lafayette and his friends heard of it directly from George III's brother, who visited the garrison at Metz in the summer of 1775, and gave a sympathetic ultra-Whig view of the conflict between the colonies and Britain. In the autumn of 1776, Lafayette and his friends, the Comte Ségur and the Vicomte Noailles, agreed to travel together to America and fight in the American cause. Their families, the ministry, and the crown disapproved of the project; Ségur and Noailles withdrew, but Lafayette persisted. On December 7, 1777, he met secretly with Silas Deane, the American agent in Paris, and signed an agreement to serve as a major-general in the American army. He did not immediately inform his family, but arranged for the secret purchase of the ship *La Bonne Mère*; he renamed the ship *La Victoire*, added the motto *Cur non?* (Why Not?) to his arms, and posted his farewell notes to his wife and his in-laws on his way to Bordeaux where he intended to embark for America in the company of some other officers who had also signed with Deane.

7 The dossier is cited in Chantal Tourtier-Bonazzi, *La Fayette: Documents conservés en France* (Paris, 1976), p. 288.

As soon as his wife's family discovered that Lafayette intended to sail, they arranged for orders from the ministry, speaking in the name of the King, to desist in his plan. Lafayette delayed his departure for a month, as he tried to determine just how serious the official opposition to his embarkation was. He concluded, finally, that he ought to carry out his original plan and his ship sailed off to America on April 20, 1777. It arrived in Charleston, South Carolina, in the middle of June; and after a month's overland journey to Philadelphia, he took a post as an unpaid volunteer on Washington's staff late in July; in September, within a week of his twentieth birthday, he was wounded at the battle of Brandywine. Revolutionary or not, he was certainly now part of the American Revolution, and he remained part of it until the end.

Did Lafayette become a revolutionary at the end of 1776, or in early 1777? Was he a revolutionary on the day he joined Washington's staff? In a memoir he wrote in 1779, he claimed that he had joined the American cause because of his attraction to and belief in America's struggle for liberty and for its independence from Britain. An attachment to such a cause would, he was sure, bring him the glory suited to his temperament, his family record and his education. Lafayette repeated those claims during a long and active life; and while he never pretended that he acted in absolute singleness and purity of motive (the chance to enter combat and to train for higher command figure as minor motifs), he nevertheless insisted that the central motive was to assist in the achievement of American liberty.

And it is that motive which Gottschalk is at pains to disprove in his *Lafayette Comes to America*, for in the preface and the conclusion Gottschalk makes it clear that it is the burden of the entire book to show how Lafayette's motives for coming to America had been the subject of a Lafayette-created myth and legend for 150 years. We are usually grateful to historians who destroy myths and legends which had paraded as historical truths, and everyone has repeated Gottschalk's conclusions on the subject ever since.

Moreover, Gottschalk provides alternative motives for Lafayette's claims. Gottschalk describes Lafayette's character and attitudes in the years immediately before the departure for America as a single constellation of frustration and hatred. Lafayette, he discovers to be a "timid and reticent adolescent," "disconsolate and unhappy," "a misfit and ill at ease among the sophisticated courtiers at Versailles and Paris"; "ill at ease and given to introspective brooding." This self-conscious lad felt "inferior and unhappy in a milieu in which his ancestry, early training and awkward manners had not prepared him," and as a "resentful youth with plenty of money" this "frustrated courtier," "hurt and humiliated by his friend and his brother-in-law" thus determined to "persevere in his plans."[8] Furthermore, he was "chiefly concerned with

8 Gottshalk, *Lafayette Comes to America*, pp. 32, 37, 38, 40, 52, 54, 56, 65, 66, 71, 73, 116.

beating the English" whom he "hated."[9] And so he sailed off to join the American Revolution. We can only pity his cabin-mates.

Thus the major premise in *Lafayette Comes to America* is that Lafayette felt impelled to leave France and join in a revolution in order to release his feelings of frustration and inferiority by (a) explicit acts of aggression against the hated English and (b) causing chagrin and dismay among the friends and relatives who had underestimated him, and thus vent aggression against them as well.

Gottschalk was using a fairly new argument for the motivation of an historical character, and he probably derived it from the work of his colleague at the University of Chicago, Harold Lasswell, whose ground-breaking *Psychopathology and Politics* had been published only a few years before the Lafayette study.[10] Lasswell was among the first of the social scientists to take a simple quasi-Freudian binary hydraulic model of the psyche, which held that "Public performance is the displaced arena for the resolution of psychic tensions."[11] This assumed that a person had "needs" or experienced "tensions" or "frustrations" which built up pressures; these were relieved by outbursts of aggression, if they were not fulfilled or "relieved" in some other way. Such activity was not irrational because, "Private motives are displaced upon public objects which are then rationalized in terms of public interest."[12] The principle that frustrations led to aggression hardened into a common paradigm shortly after John Dollard published his classic *Frustration and Aggression* in 1939,[13] and the wide acceptance of this readily understood hydraulic model of the psyche made it easy to understand and accept a thesis that Lafayette's frustrations led to aggressive and rebellious acts which he rationalized in terms of public interest.

There are two other elements in Gottschalk's thesis, not stated in his preface or conclusion, which strengthen his argument wonderfully. These are Lafayette's age and his consequent incapacity to understand the issues he later claimed he was fighting for. When Lafayette was planning to join the American Revolution he was nineteen, married three years, a father, and a veteran of three years service in the French Army. The references to him in *Lafayette Comes to America* are always as "the boy," "the youth," "the adolescent," "the stripling," or "the lad"; such references occur with increasing frequency the closer Lafayette gets to making his decision (they number 60 in the last 100 pages), and Lafayette's earnest efforts to overcome the obstacles to his departure take on an *opéra bouffe* air. He is not only a frustrated character; he is also obviously too young and immature to have motivations grounded upon anything other than visceral reactions to his immediate cir-

9 Ibid., pp. 50, 140.
10 (Chicago, 1930).
11 Lasswell, *Psychopathology and Politics*, p. 124.
12 Ibid., pp. 261-62.
13 John Dollard, et al., *Frustration and Aggression* (New Haven, 1939).

cumstances. Thus the next portion of the argument is possible. Gott-schalk comments:

> In his next epistle to Adrienne, he declares himself—somewhat prematurely—a full-fledged devotee of liberty. He had not yet stopped to think out clearly what liberty and equality might mean to him or to the world . . . but it helped to establish in his own mind a completely satisfactory rationalization of his conduct. . . . He did not really know that America was fighting for those things . . . he did not really know that liberty and equality were good. He did know that glory was good, at least for him, and since glory was to be found on the side of liberty and equality, they must be good too, especially since so many brilliant people were said to believe that they were. . . . Thus out of a few catchwords which the American agents in Paris had exploited, and the necessity for finding a rational explanation for his own extravagant conduct was born the liberalism of the foremost European exponent of the liberal creed in the two succeeding generations.[14]

When Gottschalk speaks of the American "merchant-class rebels" exploiting "catchwords," he is in the mainstream of historical thought for the mid-1930s. It seemed agreed then that the American colonists "had not taken seriously any of the ideas they spouted . . . [because] ideas and propaganda are only a mask for deeper motivations . . . [or] as Carl Becker put it, 'the colonists modified their theory to meet their needs.'"[15]

III

Louis Gottschalk's contention is that Lafayette's claim to have participated in the American Revolution on behalf of American liberty and independence is a myth and a legend. There are logical difficulties inherent in his double-barreled argument that Lafayette's real purpose was for the relief or displacement of hatred, frustration, and discontent, and that in any case he was too immature and intellectually feckless to understand the ideas of "liberty" or "equality" in any more than an incantatory way; but I shall pass them by in favor of a rejoinder on historical terms.

I argue that Lafayette was a revolutionary when he joined the American forces in 1777, on the grounds that he wilfully and self-consciously joined what he understood to be a revolution and that he shared the often reiterated goals of the majority of the leading revolutionaries in America. Implicit in my argument is the position that Lafayette's decision to come to America was not an inexplicable conversion originating in an identity crisis, nor is it most readily explained or understood in terms of his psycho-sexual development. Finally, I

14 Gottschalk, *Lafayette Comes to America*, pp. 137-38.
15 Jack Greene (ed.), *The Reinterpretations of the American Revolution* (New York, 1968), pp. 13-14. The "merchant-class rebels" appear in Gottschalk, *Lafayette Comes to America*, p. 67.

shall argue that Mme de Staël was generous but wrong-headed when she observed that "it is a singular phenomenon that such a character as M. de la Fayette should have appeared in the foremost rank of the French nobility."[16] Basic to my theme is that Lafayette's stance and his decision was not atypical for his time and his station in life.

What kind of life did Lafayette live, what values did he hold, and what elements in his temperament or character give us clues to his motives and his behavior? We might make something of the fact that he was orphaned early in life, but such a circumstance was a commonplace in the eighteenth century. We could easily find a good-sized group of public figures who had been similarly orphaned, but we have no studies which identify their common characteristics compared with public figures who had not been orphaned. If anything, the fact that his father had been killed in battle would only fortify Lafayette's sense of his destiny as a *chevalier sans peur et sans reproche* which would be fulfilled in glorious deeds on the battlefield, even unto death. We may guess that the relatives who raised him in the family chateau sustained him with stories of his proud paternal lineage and with the fact that on his mother's side he could claim descent from St. Louis; from the earliest period in his life Lafayette's correspondence shows an awareness of his membership in a heroic line connected with great moments in French military history.

But the rhetoric, language, and symbols he employed to express his hopes and dreams and his values did not originate during the early years of the French monarchy. The exalted, stagey language he used, a *lingua franca* for his contemporaries among the court nobility as well as for most literate persons in the third estate, had been fostered and cultivated during the past century by the classical curriculum in the Collèges where secondary education was offered. The Collège du Plessis fitted the standard model: in a large measure it was considered a school for character and eloquence, with lessons drawn from a limited set of eclectic Stoic poets, philosophers, and historians who wrote during the last years of the Roman Republic and the first years of the Roman Empire. Harold Parker has shown that the classical authors who were standards in the Collèges usually assumed that they were living in a decadent time; most of their praise was lavished upon an idealized Roman Republic of earlier generations during which ages, they assured their readers, men honored the pursuit of an Arcadian existence in which the virtues of justice, courage, integrity, love of country, a desire for glory, hatred of tyranny, and a willingness to sacrifice all for the sake of liberty were typical of the Roman people.[17]

16 Madame de Staël, *Considérations sur . . . la Révolution française* (Paris, 1816), Part 2, Chap. 3.
17 Harold T. Parker, *The Cult of Antiquity and the French Revolutionaries* (Chicago, 1937), pp. 22-26.

Lafayette's regular companions during the years between 1770 and 1776 were the young bloods of the court: Comte de Segur, Vicomte Noailles, Prince de Poix, Duc de La Rochfoucault, Comte Vaublanc, and the Duc de Chartres. Those whose memoirs survive show quite clearly that the young noblesse could love glory and liberty just as such disparate characters as Marat, Brissot, and Mme Roland could confide to their diaries that they were possessed by *l'amour de la gloire*. While the crown sponsored paintings for the salons which would encourage the viewer to emulate the virtues of an ancient Roman Republic, both noble and commoner saw what Durand Echeverria has called a "mirage in the west": far-off Arcadian America, where the Roman virtues were lived out in an unspoiled environment, and where a whole host of Cincinnati were ready to leave their plows and find glory in the defense of their liberties.[18]

When words like "glory" and "liberty" become the slippery coinage of accepted ideas, it is usually worth while to ask what those words meant in *that* age, rather than to make the dangerous assumption that they have the same connotations for our own era. One way to discover what these words meant would be to read some of the orations of Cicero, or that *vade mecum* of most gentlemen and public figures on both sides of the Atlantic, Cicero's *De Officiis*. Perhaps a better way to test the common collective mentality regarding these concepts is to read the ultimate repository of traditional ideas, namely, an encyclopedia.

Gloire occupies no less than five full folio pages of dense exposition in Diderot's *Encyclopédie*, and the cross-references lead the reader off to other long, related articles on *Honneur, Renommée, Considération, Estime*, and *Réputation*. What is made clear is that *gloire* is not to be confused with vainglory, with popularity, or with success. Glory supposes virtue, talents, courage, and generosity, all combined in striking actions during which great difficulties are surmounted; glory will escape the ambitious, for it assumes a "resolute soul" and a willingness to make major personal sacrifices for the public weal.[19]

Clearly, the pursuit of glory required both a noble object and a large-hearted and truly noble kind of life. More than one member of the noblesse came to America in search of glory in a noble cause in the long months before the French alliance, and the recommendations they carried with them spoke a language common to gentlemen on both sides of the Atlantic. Glory, Esteem, Honor, Fame, and Reputation were daily on the minds of the founding fathers, as Douglas Adair

18 D. Echeverria, *Mirage in the West: A History of the French Image of American Society to 1815* (Princeton, 1957). For the royal patronage of paintings showing Roman "republican" virtues, see J. Locquin, *La Peinture d'histoire en France de 1747 à 1789* (Paris, 1912).

19 *Encyclopédie, ou, Dictionnaire raisonné...* (Paris, 1751-1765), 7:716-21.

has so cogently demonstrated;[20] it was only after Nathanael Greene and George Washington were convinced that Lafayette *lived* the desire for glory he always *spoke* of, that they were ready to trust him with the command of a division, not before.

In his first command of a separate expedition in the winter of 1777-1778, Lafayette had with him nearly twenty French blue bloods, each keen about his own honor, and all hungry for glory. Perhaps none of them had read either Cicero or the *Encyclopédie*, but Lafayette never forgot that glory consisted not in success on the battlefield but in the fulfillment of a larger goal and in assisting humanity. Writing to Adrienne on his way to America, he summed it up in a few sentences:

> In striving for my own glory, I work for their happiness. . . . The welfare of America is intimately connected with the happiness of all mankind; she will become the respectable and safe asylum of virtue, integrity, tolerance, equality and peaceful liberty.[21]

But what could he possibly know about liberty, this cossetted scion of fifteen generations of continental nobility, living in a land where he was part of the apparatus of a divine right kingship? What indeed? One is reminded of the exchange between Sam Adams and another French volunteer in the America Revolution. Age seventeen and only a week in America, Pierre Du Ponceau met Sam Adams in Boston in December, 1777. The newcomer said he had always been a stern Republican.

> When Samuel Adams discovered my Republican principles, he was astonished. "Where," he said to me, "did you learn all that?" "In France," replied I. "In France! That is impossible!" Then, recovering himself, he added, "Well, because a man was born in a stable, it is no reason why he should be a horse."[22]

If Sam Adams was surprised to find any Frenchman with a knowledge of republican principles, Silas Deane was pleased by the reception he received as the American agent in Paris. The Declaration of Independence had reached France only a few months before, and Deane wrote to John Jay:

> I have a levee of officers and others every morning as numerous if not as splendid, as a prime minister. Indeed I have had occasionally dukes, marquesses, and even bishops and counts and chevaliers without number, all of whom are jealous, being out of employ here or having friends they wish to advance in the cause of liberty.[23]

20 Douglas Adair, *Fame and the Founding Fathers* (New York, 1974); see also R. M. Gummere, *The American Colonial Mind and the Classical Tradition* (Cambridge, 1963).
21 June 7, 1777, Cornell University: *Dean Collection*.
22 J. L. Whitehead (ed.), "The Autobiography of Peter Stephen Du Ponceau," *Pennsylvania Magazine of History and Biography*, 63 (1939), 201.
23 December 2, 1776, in L. Bendikson, "Restoration of Secret Writing," *Franco-American Review* (1937), 248; similar comments by Deane in August and November, 1776, are in his correspondence in *The Deane Papers*, New York Historical Society Collections, 1886, 1:211, 342.

Surely there were mountebanks, mercenaries, and other fakes among the crowds at Deane's levees; and doubtless some wished to go to America because it afforded an opportunity to avoid something in France. But were they all providing rationalizations for other motives than those they declared? If they acquiesced in a polity which was less than wholly free or completely equal, did it follow that they were incapable of understanding liberty? Did one have to be a closeted *philosophe* to understand the rudiments of the Americans' stated goals?

We have a complex enough understanding today of the French nobility to be aware that when they spoke positively of "liberty" they could mean a form of the "liberties" which were privileges held by charter or by tradition, or they could mean freedom from arbitrary, despotic, or tyrannical government, or even government which operated outside of traditional and accepted frames of customary law. The *Parlements* adverted to this theme often during the eighteenth century. A commitment to their own liberty and an opposition to real or imagined tyranny was part of a common classical heritage of the European nobility and part of their historical memory. It happened that it was also the heritage of the leaders of the American Revolution who, in their Declaration of Independence, spoke not about the depredations of the British Parliament but against the "asbolute tyranny" and "absolute despotism" of the Crown. Even Louis XVI, to say nothing of George III, could be shocked by that; in fact, it was Frederick the Great who remarked to his Ambassador to London that "the treatment the colonies are receiving seems to me the first steps towards despotism."[24]

Again, the *Encyclopédie* may provide an index of the commonplace status of a set of ideas, even if the reader had not attended a Collège. There are ten full, consecutive pages in the *Encyclopédie* on *Liberté*, with the following subheads: *morale*, *naturelle*, *de penser*, *civile*, and *politique*, the whole ending with a fine peroration from Montesquieu.[25] While few of Lafayette's fellow officers were bookish, they did read the *nouvelles écrites* from Paris, and they shared in the talk at the Masonic Lodge at Metz; a few lunched with Abbé Raynal when they were in Paris. Ségur reports that, "Liberty, whatever its language, appealed to us by its courage, as equality did by its convenience," and he gives an account of the great wave of sympathy among his peers as they saw "liberty fighting so bravely against tyranny."[26] Of course, both Ségur and

24 Paul L. Haworth, "Frederick the Great and the American Revolution," *American Historical Review*, 9 (1903), 462.
25 *Encyclopédie* . . . , 9:462-72.
26 *Mémoires du Comte de Ségur* (Paris, 1890), p. 27; for the "new writings from Paris," *Mémoires de M. Le Comte de Vaublanc* (Paris; 1857), p. 79; for the attendance of Lafayette and his friends at the meetings of the Masonic Lodges, see L. Gottschalk, *Lafayette and the Close of the American Revolution* (Chicago, 1942), pp. 433-34; the lunches with Raynal, *Mémoires du . . . Ségur*, p. 66; and in a letter of October 1, 1777, Lafayette reminds Adrienne of conversations with Raynal.

Noailles intended to be companions of Lafayette on his voyage to
America, but they lacked both his independent means and his capacity
for independent action. The Comte Vaublanc remembered when
Lafayette first announced plans to fight on the side of liberty in
America: he was with a group of officers at a dinner at La
Rochefoucault's. "The officers crowded around Lafayette and heaped
him with praises. The word liberty resounded through our conversations; he was going to contribute to its restoration among a great
people."[27]

It seems clear that the notion of "liberty" was both widespread and
reasonably well understood among many of the young aristocrats of
Lafayette's circle, and it did not seem strange to many Frenchmen to go
to America and fight in that cause. Their motives may not have been
completely unsullied by secondary considerations, but it appears that
the chief reason that many of them wanted to go was that they wished to
be engaged in the support of a "glorious" cause which could restore
liberty to a people who seemed underdogs in their struggle. For all of
this, Lafayette served as a popular model by the autumn of 1777.

IV

There is a final question which may not be answerable to everyone's
satisfaction: is there adequate positive evidence to support a contention
that Lafayette joined the American Revolution on its own terms in
1777? Taking into account the published psychological analyses of
revolutionaries of every stripe during the past quarter-century, is it not
more probable that his motives really were personal discontent, frustration, and hatred of the English? What is required before anything
else is some concrete evidence that those negative motives really did
operate. By almost any worldly standards of his time, Lafayette in his
nineteenth year could be envied by many young men of his social class:
he had more unencumbered wealth at his immediate disposal than
most of them; he had married into a powerful and influential family
which had made regular efforts to forward his career in the directions
he hoped it would go; his correspondence with his father-in-law shows
a mixture of respect and affection which could lead us to think he had
found a satisfactory surrogate father; his marriage was stable and
Adrienne was the very epitome of the devoted wife; he seemed to enjoy
the company of his friends in the social life typical of his age and class.[28]

27 *Mémoires de M. le Comte de Vaublanc* (Paris, 1857), p. 79.
28 Lafayette's letters to his wife from London, cited below, and the constant flow of
   references to his numerous friends in Paris in the letters from America indicate
   clearly that he was never a social recluse, and that he enjoyed the company of his set.
   All of these letters have appeared in the documentary collections, Stanley J. Idzerda
   (ed.), *Lafayette in the Age of the American Revolution: Selected Letters and Papers, 1776-
   1790*, 3 vols. (Ithaca and London: Cornell University Press, 1977, 1979, 1980).

Lafayette seems to have had more reasons for staying in France than most noblemen of his age and condition; he chose instead to face the awesome risks of an Atlantic crossing and of joining with a people whose anti-French prejudices were solidly based upon two centuries of ignorance. What follows is a review of his own statements of his reasons for going to America; they seem to reiterate a consistent pattern of goals and motives. If one wishes to show that whenever he says one thing, he really means something else, the burden is upon him to demonstrate Lafayette's unwitting duplicity.

The tone of Lafayette's correspondence in 1777 differs very little, if at all, from that found in the bulk of the nearly 5,000 extant letters he wrote up to 1834. They are ingenious and transparent, sometimes to an aggravating degree; and while Lafayette seems always to wish to ingratiate himself with his correspondent, it is also clear that he intends to do what is necessary to meet his own standards of conduct and his own view of his destiny.

The first letter we have in which Lafayette speaks of his departure for America is to William Carmichael, Silas Deane's secretary, dated February 11, 1777; in it he informs Carmichael that he has just completed the purchase of a ship and that "in a month at the latest, I hope to be able to take to your country the zeal which animates me for their happiness, their glory, and their liberty."[29] As he left Paris for embarkation at Bordeaux (with the expectation that he would be out to sea within a week), he wrote a hasty note to his father-in-law, the Duc d'Ayen, telling him, for the first time, that he was leaving for America despite the disapproval of his family and the government. The letter begins: "You will be astonished, my dear Papa, by what I am about to tell you," and after some further apologies for not consulting him, Lafayette adds a detail that might mollify any father-in-law: "I have found a unique opportunity to distinguish myself and to learn my profession"; and then the bombshell: "I am a general officer in the army of the United States of America. My zeal for their cause, and my sincerity have won their confidence. On my side, I have done everything I could for them, and their interests will always be more dear to me than my own."[30]

Of course, Lafayette was not able to get away as quickly as he hoped, for D'Ayen pressed the ministry to take official steps to stop his son-in-law, requiring him to give up his project. Nearly a month went by, as he contended with the efforts of his in-laws and French officialdom to thwart his departure. If he had seen the "*ordre du Roi*" enjoining all French officers on their way to the Antilles to desist in their plans to join the American forces, "and notably to the Marquis de la Fayette who

29 Papers of William Carmichael, U.S. National Archives: RG 233, HR 27A-G7.4, Tray 742, item 98.
30 Dated March 9, 1777, with a postscript written on March 16, Cornell University: *Dean Collection*.

is to return to France immediately," he might have obeyed it, but it remained wrapped in red tape in the Marine ministry.[31] On April 19th, he wrote one final letter to Carmichael and reminded him that "the only favor" he asked of the Americans "is that they give me every possible opportunity to make use of my fortune, my labors, and all the resources of my imagination, and to shed my blood for my brothers and my friends."[32] And then a farewell note to Adrienne: many protestations about the pain of parting, many reassurances that he would not be hurt in America, and one last assurance concerning the atttempts to keep him from joining the Revolution across the water: "having to choose between the slavery which everyone believes they have a right to impose upon me, and Liberty, which called me to glory, I departed."[33] His ship sailed the next day.

They were nearly two months at sea. Lafayette whiled away his time keeping a lookout for English cruisers and studying military tactics and English; occasionally he added a new passage in a long letter to Adrienne:

> As the defender of that liberty which I idolize, freer than anyone else, coming as a friend to offer my services to this most interesting republic, I bring there only my sincerity and my good will, and no personal ambition or selfish interest. In striving for my own glory, I work for their happiness. I trust that, for my sake, you will become a good American. Besides, it is a sentiment made for virtuous hearts. The welfare of America is intimately connected with the happiness of all mankind; she will become the respectable and safe asylum of virtue, integrity, tolerance, equality and a peaceful liberty.[34]

Not content with emptying his heart to Adrienne, he apparently tried to make some of his fellow passengers "good Americans." When the Comte Mauroy expressed some reservations about the total idealism of the embattled farmers under Washington, he reports that Lafayette was quick with a rejoinder:

> "Eh, what," he said to me one day, "don't you believe that the people are united by the love of virtue and liberty? Don't you believe that they are simple, good, hospitable people who prefer beneficence to all our vain pleasures, and death to slavery?"[35]

The final paragraph of the letter to Adrienne was written at the end of Lafayette's first day in America and sent from Major Huger's plantation home near Georgetown, South Carolina; he was overjoyed to report that the experience of twenty-four hours confirmed his

31 H. Doniol, *Histoire de la participation de la France à l'établissement des Etats-Unis d'Amérique* (Paris, 1886), 2:395, n. 2.
32 Papers of William Carmichael. See n. 29: tray 742, item 99.
33 April 19, 1777, Cornell University: *Dean Collection*.
34 June 7, 1777, Cornell University: *Dean Collection*.
35 This is from an account Mauroy wrote upon his return to France in 1779. Archives nationales: Affaires étrangères, 219, fols. 1-2.

expectations: "The manners of the people are simple, honest, and in every way worthy of this land where everything proclaims the beautiful name of *liberty*."[36]

Five days later he wrote to Adrienne from Charleston, his enthusiasm undimmed by the rigors of a seventy-five-mile hike from Georgetown, the swarms of gnats, and the bad water, all of which his companions remembered as an ordeal. What struck Lafayette was "the openness of the inhabitants" and

> the affinity between their way of thinking and my own . . . and for glory and liberty. . . . They are as likeable as my enthusiasm has led me to picture them. A simplicity of manners, a desire to please, a love of country and liberty, and an easy equality prevail everywhere here . . . although there are some immense fortunes in this country, I challenge anyone to discover the slightest difference in their manners toward each other.[37]

Surely this was the Rome of Regulus and Cincinnatus!

The long trip north to Philadelphia took nearly a month, and Lafayette's little party was to discover that America had no need of their services: Congress was already swamped with French volunteers. Without wasting his time in recriminations, Lafayette pressed his claim to serve as a volunteer without pay, and he was given a commission on July 31. Two weeks later he wrote, in English, a letter to John Hancock, the President of the Congress, accepting his commission with a lofty sweep of rhetoric Hancock surely understood.

> The feelings of my heart, long before it became my duty, engaged me in the love of the American cause. I not only considered it was the cause of Honor, Virtue and universal happiness, but felt myself impressed with the warmest affection for a Nation who exhibited by their resistance so fine an example of Justice and courage to the Universe.[38]

Lafayette had been told by Congressman Lovell in July that he could not serve in the American army; now that he was an American major-general, Lafayette's syntax revealed how far he had come by August 21, when he wrote Lovell recommending a commission for Casimir Pulaski, "the most dangerous enemy of the tyrants of his country," who (with a sudden slip into a common possessive pronoun) "is asking leave of fighting for our liberty."[39] If Adrienne was not yet an "American," Lafayette had hastened to become one, for he commonly referred to "we," "us," and "our" when speaking of American interests during the rest of his career in his adopted country.

In the weeks after the battle of Brandywine, Lafayette had time to write longer letters home; he was recovering from his wound in the Moravian hospital in Bethlehem. It is from that hospital bed that we

36 June 5, 1777, Cornell University: *Dean Collection*.
37 June 19, 1777, Cornell University: *Dean Collection*.
38 August 13, 1777, U.S. National Archives: RG 360, PCC 156, 1-4.
39 August 21, 1777, U.S. National Archives: RG 360, PCC 41, 8, 27.

hear, for the *first* time, of his rancor against the English. As he assures Adrienne that he cannot leave the war just to attend a ball in Paris, he reminds her "it is not for such pleasure that I would abandon an army fighting both for liberty and against the English."[40] As the months wear on, his response to England becomes stronger, and in later letters to the Duc d'Ayen and to Adrienne he settles down to his standard description of "arrogant" and "insolent" England, as in his letter of January 6, 1778:

> I have a great desire to see this revolution succeed. The humiliation of insolent England, the advantage to my country, the welfare of humanity, for which it is important that there be in the world a people who are entirely free, and the sacrifices that I and my friends have already made for this cause.[41]

Yet when Lafayette had visited England in February, 1777 (when he already knew he was going to leave for America), his letters to Adrienne are full of happy references to the kindly treatment he received and what a delightful city London was; even though he mentioned that he expected France and England would soon be at war, he showed no animus whatever toward either the English people or the English nation. Indeed, animus or hatred was utterly out of character for Lafayette. If we examine his attitudes toward the English over the years from late 1777 to 1783, we find that he shared with his American hosts a sense of outrage concerning English insensitivities in dealing with America; with their boasts that they would easily destroy the rag-tag American army, and their treatment of American prisoners and non-combatants. What may have been merely stupid or incompetent in the English conduct of the war, Lafayette and many of the American revolutionaries found "insolent" and "arrogant." By the time Lafayette wrote his memoirs in 1779 he readily referred to the "pride" and "arrogance" of the English, but nowhere does he indicate that those epithets he learned in America motivated him to leave France in the spring of 1777.[42]

Before his first six months of service were completed, Lafayette had his division. De Kalb wrote to Europe that Lafayette was "a prodigy for his age. He is the model of valor, intelligence, judgment, good-conduct, generosity and zeal for the cause of liberty for this continent."[43] Lafayette was ready to admit his earlier naïveté: he was shocked by the neutrality practiced by the Quakers, and he confessed

40 October 29, 1977, Idzerda, *Lafayette in the Age of the American Revolution*, 1, 138.
41 January 6, 1778, Cornell University: *Dean Collection*.
42 The five letters from London were written during his visit as a guest of the French ambassador, Adrienne's uncle. Lafayette already knew he was going to America: when he returned to France early in March, 1777, he headed for his ship at Bordeaux. Archives La Grange: Comte René Chambrun Collection.
43 De Kalb to Saint-Paul, November 7, 1777, in *American Historical Review*, 15 (1910), 563.

to Washington, "When I was in Europe I thought that here almost every man was a lover of liberty and would rather die free than live slave. You can conceive my astonishment when I saw that Toryism was as openly professed as Whigism itself."[44] Nonetheless, he remained undaunted in his original mission and in his readiness to sacrifice himself for a cause in which he believed. Although he remained a patriotic Frenchman (he was ready to return home in a moment if his own country was at war), he fell into the American habit of identifying the country with the cause, as when he commented to Henry Laurens, "I want more to serve America and the cause of liberty and mankind than to be thanked for those services."[45]

On the face of it then, Lafayette consistently expressed his motives for coming to America and for staying there for the sake of the glory attached to the achievement of liberty. He considered the American cause one that was pregnant with the future of mankind, and he was not the only one in America or Europe who expressed such ideas. There remains the possibility that he was subject to a massive continuing self-deception, a common enough syndrome among talented and strong-willed persons. Yet he lived among a group of American officers, each of whom was jealous of his rank and prerogatives, and most of whom were ready to accuse others of outrageous behavior or motivation when a conflict of rank or interest arose. None of the memorials of American officers and none of the letters or memoirs of those with whom he served in the American Revolution ever suggest any criticism of Lafayette other than that he had a touchy sense of honor: indeed, in complaints made about foreign officers, Lafayette was specifically mentioned as an exception.[46] Most of the memoirs of Lafayette's contemporaries in the French court are unfriendly to Lafayette, for most of them assume that if he did not betray the King during the French Revolution, at the least he failed to seize the opportunity to save the royal family in 1792. Despite the cool or negative response to him in these memoirs, none suggest that Lafayette came to America because of frustration, discontent, or any other malaise.

We are thus brought to face the myth and the legend that Lafayette came to America because of frustration, discontent, and hatred for the English, a myth created in 1935 by Gottschalk's *Lafayette Comes to America*. While it intended to destroy an earlier interpretation, Gottschalk's book created for us a new myth and legend which has

---

44 December 30, 1777, Lafayette College: *Hubbard Collection*.
45 December 14, 1777, South Carolina Historical Society: Laurens Papers.
46 See the memorial of American officers on January 2, 1778, in *Letters and Papers of Major General John Sullivan*, 1:606-608, and the letter of Washington to Gouverneur Morris, July 24, 1778: "I do most devoutly wish, that we had not a single foreigner among us, except the Marquis de Lafayette, who acts upon very different principles from those which govern the rest." *Writings of George Washington* (Washington, D.C., 1934), 12:227-28.

served us well, if the texts and reference books are any judge. Since
many historians of the American Revolution of the last generation
rediscovered that an intense appetite for liberty was one of the fundamental reasons why so many Americans were willing to risk their lives,
their fortunes, and their sacred honor in the years 1776 to 1783,[47] it
may be that time has come for us to reassess Lafayette's original claims
that he was risking his life and his honor in the same cause for the same
reasons, and to conclude that he became a revolutionary in 1777 on
behalf of America's struggle for political liberty.

47 See the discussion of the work of Bailyn, Morgan, Wood, et al., in Greene, *Reinterpretations*, pp. 38ff.

Conrad-Alexandre Gérard and the Coming of the Revolution in Alsace

RUTH STRONG HUDSON

The demand for the convocation of the Estates-General to solve the deepening economic and financial crises of France in 1787 and 1788 raised the lid on a Pandora's box of vexations relative to procedure. Traditionally, local and provincial assemblies sitting separately in the constituted orders of society (clergy, nobility, and third estate) had selected delegates to the Estates-General and drawn up the *cahiers de doléances*, or statements of grievances to be reviewed and redressed by that body. Certain provinces, however, such as Alsace, had no precedent for the business of selecting delegates and drawing up the *cahiers*, for they had been "reunited to the Crown"[1] (in the terminology of the day), after the last meeting of the Estates-General in 1614.

Having never been represented either in her own estates or the Estates-General, Alsace remained the "tranquil spectator of the afflicting scenes in other provinces,"[2] wrote the *préteur royal* of Strasbourg. All through the great debate on voting by chamber or by head, while provincial assemblies were torn by dissension and parlements revolted in half a dozen cities of France, she "awaited in silence the general decision"[3] on representation in the Estates.

The *préteur*, Conrad-Alexandre Gérard, attributed the calm prevailing in his native province to "the phlegmatic character of her inhabitants,"[4] but there was more than German stolidity beneath that

---

1 The policy of *réunion* implying the return to the central kingdom of territories illegally usurped by feudal lords was implemented by special courts created to search out those territories in Alsace and the Three Bishoprics. Other provinces incorporated by France in the seventeenth century were Flanders, Artois, and Rousillon, following the Treaty of the Pyrenees (1659), and the Free county of Burgundy and the Cambrésis, following the Treaty of Nimwegen (1678).

2 [Conrad-Alexandre Gérard], *Projet d'instructions pour le chapitre de ... à l'Assemblée du District*, 1789 (n.p.), p. 8. On the title page the words *de Neuviller* are handwritten between brackets following the words *le chapitre*.

3 Ibid., p. 8.

4 Ibid., p. 18. Cf. the comment in a recent study of political life in Alsace just before and during the Revolution: the Alsatian citizen "by his concern for order and moderation, by his refusal to become extremist, by the absence of hostile sentiment toward either rural or city dwellers as a class ... stands in sharp contrast to many of his compatriots of the 'interior.'" Roland Marx, *Recherches sur la vie politique de l'Alsace prérévolutionnaire et révolutionnaire* (Strasbourg, 1966), p. 178.

calm. To begin with, Alsace was physically remote, separated from the "interior," as the rest of France was (and still is) known, by the Vosges Mountains. Before the advent of steam, the trip by stagecoach from Paris to Strasbourg lasted twelve days; couriers on horseback, of course, could make it in less, and the record of four days would be set by the rider who brought the news of the fall of the Bastille. Although the Rhine was nominally the eastern boundary of Alsace, the great river served far more as an artery, linking the province with other parts of the Rhineland, to which it was culturally and commercially oriented. As part of the eastern frontier Alsace was not only distant from the central government in Versailles, it also bore a peculiar and anomalous relationship to the Monarchy. Although a conquered province, Alsace continued until the Revolution to invoke former privileges and immunities based on the "Germanic liberties" which had long been a favorite topic of writers on jurisprudence.

The special status of Alsace was the price paid by the Monarchy for rolling the frontier back to the Rhine. *Clausa Germanis Gallia* read the inscription on Molart's[5] medal struck by order of the Sun King in 1683, when the star-shaped citadel of Vauban was erected to cut off access from the Rhine to Strasbourg. Two years before, the Imperial Free City of Strasbourg, beleaguered by the armies of Louvois, had accepted "voluntary submission" in exchange for the guarantee of numerous prerogatives in the Articles of Capitulation. Thus was completed the process of *réunion*, initiated in 1648 by the Treaty of Münster, which ceded the Habsburg holdings in Alsace, the fortress of Breisach, and the cities of the Decapole[6] to His Most Christian Majesty. The ambiguous, indeed contradictory, terms of the cessions were followed by thirty years of juridical discussion, negotiation, coercion, wars, subsequent treaties, and the eventual Capitulation of Strasbourg.

By the end of the seventeenth century, France was in virtual control of Alsace; yet one-sixth to one-third of the population,[7] inhabiting several hundred seigneuries, ecclesiastical properties, and villages

---

5 Michel Molart (1641-1713), medalist, sculptor in ivory, born in Dieppe, called to Paris by Louvois, and commissioned to commemorate various events of the reign. The name sometimes appears as Molard or Mollart.

6 The Decapole was a defensive league of city-states administered under the Empire by a *landvogt*. The ten member cities were Landau, Wissembourg, Haguenau, Rosheim, Obernai, Séléstat, Colmar, Kaysersberg, Türckheim, and Münster. The fortress of Breisach on the right bank was considered the military key to Alsace: it was returned to the Empire by the Treaty of Ryswick (1697) and a new fortress city called Neuf-Brisach built on the left bank by Vauban.

7 [Gérard], *Projet d'instructions*, p. 21: "a large part of the province (about one-sixth) belongs by virtue of existing treaties to foreign princes, who spend the income from their estates outside Alsace, without paying taxes in the province." Modern historians have estimated as high as one-third of the inhabitants to be subjects of foreign princes. Alsace in 1789 consisted of 1,442 territories, as listed in "L'Alsace féodale, Etat de cette province en 1789," Jacques Baquol, *L'Alsace ancienne et moderne, ou dictionnaire topographique, historique et statistique du Haut et du Bas-Rhin* (Strasbourg, 1865), pp. 609-31.

continued to pay their feudal dues to princes and prelates of the Empire. The directive ascribed to Louis XIV, *"il ne faut pas toucher aux affaires de l'Alsace,"* imposing a hands-off policy, has often been interpreted as applying to the province generally. However, the original reference was to the foreign (non-French) princes and their numerous holdings, which would constitute, along with the mixture of populations and the mixture of religions, one of the great problems of Alsace at the approach of the Revolution.[8]

With regard to the diversity in religion, however, court policy was anything but hands off. Although the countryside had remained about two-thirds Catholic, Strasbourg had an almost solidly Lutheran population and an outstanding university dedicated to the instruction of youth within the framework of the Confession of Augsburg. Both were an affront to the King's fanaticism, to be treated with various forms of pressure, discrimination, and persecution, all sources of bitterness.

At the top of the politico-military administration superimposed on the province were the governor-general, the provincial commander of nearly ten thousand troops garrisoned in Strasbourg, and the intendant with his extensive powers of police, justice, and finance. The ten cities of the Decapole and, after the Capitulation, Strasbourg were forced to accept into their deliberations an offical known as *préteur royal*, who was given a multitude of supervisory functions, plus the power of absolute veto. In the seigneuries, on the other hand, where local life was most intense, "the representatives of the central power (regents) were nearly lost in the antheap of seigneurial and communal organisms dating from the Middle Ages."[9]

Judicial procedures remained much the same, except for a ruling that court hearings and other public affairs were to be conducted in French, and this was largely ignored. Since the privilege of *committimus* was expressly forbidden in Alsace, litigants could not be dragged to Paris before unfamiliar judges proceeding in unfamiliar ways. They were heard before their own tribunals, with the right of appeal to the Sovereign Council of Alsace, which sat at Colmar continuously from 1698 to 1789—as jealous of its own prerogatives as of the Alsatian liberties it sought to defend.

Commercially Alsace continued to share in the rich traffic of the Rhineland, being in a sort of no man's land known as *pays à l'instar de l'étranger effectif*, now within, now without the customs barrier of France which ended with the Vosges. This did not, of course, preclude the establishment of the Five General Farms in the province, despite the difficulty of finding agents who were fluent in both French and German. In cultural matters a line of demarcation persisted at least until the middle of the eighteenth century, when the old German habits of

8 [Gérard], *Projet d'instructions*, pp. 18, 19.
9 Rodolphe Reuss, *Histoire d'Alsace* (Paris, 1912), p. 120.

thought, custom, and speech began imperceptibly to mingle with those of the invader.[10]

The royal praetors (*préteurs*) of the Decapole and of Strasbourg were usually Alsatians by birth, and often men of parts and distinction, with an occasional rascal thrown in. The first *préteur* of Strasbourg, Ulrich Obrecht,[11] was a professor at the university, and a Lutheran, as all its professors had to be and were, without exception, until the Revolution.[12] In the fall of 1684, Obrecht went to Versailles for orientation in his new role; in the spring of 1685, he returned a Catholic. The consternation of the Magistracy was matched only by the despair of his family and friends.

Several decades later, the incumbent *préteur*, François Joseph de Klinglin, exploited his office with such engaging effrontery, daring, and imagination that he has been called "one of the most interesting scoundrels . . . in the administrative annals of the old regime."[13] Klinglin was impresario for a five-day extravaganza in honor of the visit of Louis le Bien-Aimé to the Royal Free City in 1744, dazzling the visitors and populace with brilliant entertainments, fireworks, water games on the River Ill, free wine and beer, all at the expense of the Magistracy. In the end, Klinglin was investigated by Versailles; he died in prison before his trial, unable to clear himself of misdeeds which he was not the first to commit, but for which he was the first to be called to account.

Less colorful, if more conscientious, the last of the *préteurs* was Conrad-Alexandre Gérard (1729-90), native of Masevaux in Upper Alsace.[14] His father was feudal administrator of the Rottembourg estates which were later added to those of the Rosen clan, making their

10 It was in the 1740s that the French language began to be taught in a few schools. Franklin L. Ford in *Strasbourg in Transition* (Cambridge, Massachusetts, 1958), p. 171, speaks of the "social and cultural watershed" of the mid-eighteenth century in Strasbourg. Louis Adolphe Spach in *Oeuvres choisies* (Paris, Strasbourg, 1866), 3: 431ff., gives a fascinating description of the changes taking place in the city seventy odd years after its Capitulation.

11 Ulrich Obrecht (1646-1701), member of the Magistracy, erudite scholar, and author of numerous works on jurisprudence. While *préteur*, Obrecht was responsible for the introduction of the *alternative*, or alternation of Catholics and Protestants in municipal office, a source of great anguish to the Magistracy. An attempt to introduce the *alternative* into the selection of University professors in the mid-eighteenth century was thwarted by the vigilance and influence of the most distinguished Alsatian scholar of the day, Jean-Daniel Schoepflin (1694-1771), who was named Historiographer of the King in 1739, six years before Voltaire received his appointment to the same post.

12 Christian Pfister, *Pages alsaciennes* (Strasbourg and Paris, 1927), p. 240. Catholic students were admitted early in the eighteenth century. The regulations governing the most minute phases of university life are analyzed at length by Rodolphe Reuss, "Les Statuts de l'ancienne Université de Strasbourg," *Revue d'Alsace* (1873), 433ff.

13 Ford, *Strasbourg in Transition*, p. 84.

14 The division into Upper Alsace (southern) and Lower Alsace (northern) for administrative purposes is as old as the Carolingians, and still obtains in the departments of Haut-Rhin and Bas-Rhin created by the Revolution.

joint heirs among the most extensive landholders in Alsace. The seigneur of Masevaux at the time Gérard was born there was Conrad-
Alexandre de Rottembourg, who gave the child his name and the
example of a career in diplomacy.[15] But Gérard's first vocation and
predominating concern in all his endeavors was the law. He took a
doctorate in jurisprudence at the University of Strasbourg and was
named avocat to the *Conseil Souverain* before serving two stints as
embassy secretary in Mannheim and in Vienna. In 1766 he was
brought back to Versailles to head one of the Political Bureaus in the
Department of Foreign Affairs. In this capacity, ten years later when
France began secretly aiding the American Revolution, Gérard super-
vised the handling of requests from the American commissioners in
Paris for war materiel, money, and naval stores. In January, 1778,
Gérard was empowered to negotiate the Treaties of Commerce and
Alliance on behalf of France, and was granted a patent of nobility as
Count de Munster, a title which he virtually never used. Two months
later he sailed for Philadelphia as the first accredited diplomatic repre-
sentative of any nation to the United States.

Following Gérard's return to France, François Baron d'Autigny
decided to relinquish the office of *préteur royal* of Strasbourg in order to
have more time for cultural activities and his salon. Gérard was an
obvious candidate, as he already held the post of royal syndic of
Strasbourg, which was frequently a stepping stone to the praetorship.
His wide acquaintance in court and administrative circles would be
useful to him, and his connections in Alsace with the University, the
Sovereign Council, and the landed aristocracy would recommend him
to the Magistracy. The functions of the *préteur* had changed somewhat,
but the office was still highly prestigious, and not unbecoming a former
minister plenipotentiary whose services had been rewarded with the
honorific but enviable title of *conseiller d'état*.

Gérard was appointed in March, 1781, sworn in on April 2 before
the Sovereign Council, and duly installed in his functions by their
representative on the fifth. One of his first official duties was to plan
and preside over the three-day celebration, in September, of Strasbourg's centenary as a Royal Free City of France. It was one of those
elaborate festivals so dear to the Alsatian heart, complete with church
pageantry, banquets, illuminations, fireworks, official speeches, a play
commissioned by Gérard for the occasion, and the striking of a com-
memorative medal by J.-M. Weis, II.[16] Two mass weddings were per-

15 Conrad Alexandre, comte de Rottembourg (1684-1735), was a grandson of Conrad
   de Rosen, Saint-Simon's "seigneur of Bollwiller," one of the generals of Louis XIV
   and *maréchal de France*. Rottembourg served in several diplomatic missions, including
   one in Madrid where he negotiated the first Family Compact (1733) between the
   Bourbon monarchies of France and Spain.
16 Johann-Martin Weis (1738-1807), second of his name to enrich the history of Strasbourg with engravings of local scenes and happenings, did the illustrations for J.-A.

formed, one in the Cathedral and one in the Lutheran sanctuary of the Temple-Neuf, and a dowry provided for each of the twenty virtuous young brides chosen from the Tribes (guilds) of the bourgeoisie.

During his eight years as *préteur*, Gérard dealt constantly with the Magistracy, and in his contention with their Councils frequently opposed the wishes of some or all of their members. However, in his correspondence with the court, particularly the Marquis de Ségur, the Minister for War, within whose competence lay the affairs of Alsace, he made himself the "voice" or instrument of the Magistracy.[17] Yet his concerns went far beyond theirs; he defended the interests of such a variety of groups that he appears as the advocate of the entire province.

In a barrage of letters to the ministers he opposes the Royal General Farm's repeated attempts to encroach upon the rich customs collections of Strasbourg.[18] He protests the billeting of officers on the civilian population,[19] the recruiting of soldiers by German princes in Kehl, just across the Rhine, which brings the efforts of England (with whom France was still at war in America) to raise troops in Germany "to the very gates of Strasbourg."[20] He informs Ségur that the Magistracy of Strasbourg will offer the King a contribution of 100,000 livres to "help repair the losses" suffered by the navy in the war, and the guild of merchants is offering its own "special free gift" of 12,000 livres, both of which Ségur is to carry "to the foot of the throne."[21] Then a terrible fire occurs in Strasbourg, hundreds of people are burned out and homeless, and Gérard seeks assistance for them; part of the sum offered by the Magistracy to the Navy would later be diverted to the relief of the victims of the fire.[22]

Silbermann, *Local-Geschichte der Stadt Strassburg* (1775) and many other illustrations and medals. His father, J.-M. Weis, I (1711-1751) is particularly known for his series of eleven engravings minutely depicting the festivities staged by Klinglin in honor of the King's visit in 1744.

17 Gérard to Joli de Fleury, Strasbourg, May, 1782, Archives communales de la ville de Strasbourg antérieures à 1790, *Inventaire sommaire rédigé par J. Brucker, archiviste*, Série AA, Actes constitutifs et politiques de la commune, Première Partie (Strasbourg, 1878), Archives du Préteur Royal, Fonds Gérard, AA 2657, no. 80. The following citations from Gérard's correspondence with the court are all from this source; only the volume numbers, AA 2657 and AA 2658, are cited here.

18 Gérard to Ségur, Versailles, May 1, 1781, AA 2657, no. 7; Gérard to Ségur, Strasbourg, January 31, 1782, AA 2657, no. 51; Gérard to Fleury, March 18, 1783, AA 2658, fol. 10-29; Gérard to several ministers, AA 2658, fol. 64-68, and to Ségur, Paris, November 7, 1783, AA 2658, fol. 76. In October, 1783, he redoubled his efforts, writing both to Ségur and Vergennes on October 12 and October 17, to d'Ormesson on the seventeenth and to Lavoisier, then in the Royal General Farm, on the fifteenth.

19 Gérard to Ségur, Versailles, June 14, 1781, AA 2657, no. 18.

20 Gérard to Vergennes and Ségur, February 21, 1781, AA 2657, no. 59. Gérard to Vergennes, Strasbourg, March 6, 1782, AA 2657, no. 65.

21 Gérard to Ségur, Strasbourg, June 22, 1782, AA 2657, no. 88.

22 Gérard to Joli de Fleury, Paris, November 23, 1782, AA 2657, no. 105, also no. 99 to Fleury, no. 106 to Ségur.

When the *péage corporel*[23] of the Jews is being discussed in Versailles before its abolition (1784), Gérard makes a lengthy analysis of usges and customs pertaining to Jews, and their legal status in Strasbourg and Germany. He follows it up with letters to six different court officials urging abolition of the toll with some form of indemnification of the Magistracy for loss of income from that source.[24] He furthers the establishment of a workshop for the weaving of local wool and making it into sheets in an empty wing of the Foundling Home in Strasbourg, which will serve to teach the children a useful trade and help reduce indigency.[25] He is proud of having sponsored the founding of a bilingual gazette "by a group of literary people and university professors of the city." The German edition will spread the works of French authors east of the Rhine, and the French edition will "make known in France the riches of German literature."[26]

In February, 1787, Gérard received a summons from the King to the Assembly of Notables in Versailles. He and the twenty-three other "municipal heads" of cities throughout France were on the bottom rung of the glittering array of dignitaries, robe and sword, princes of the church and of the blood, invited by Calonne to hear his proposals for reform. The Notables, predictably, refused to tax themselves, but the decision to create assemblies in provinces which had none was of importance to Alsace.

An aristocratic provincial assembly met in Strasbourg in August, 1787, and again in November, named an intermediary commission to collect information, and set in motion the machinery for communal and district assemblies. The *procès-verbal* stated that "the province of

23 Foreign Jews entering the province had to pay a toll known as the *péage corporel* for the privilege of using the King's highways, and were obliged to show the receipt upon demand in taverns, lodging houses, etc. Jews domiciled in the province of Alsace were also required to pay toll, renewable every seven days, for themselves as well as for the merchandise they carried. Sometimes transmuted into a yearly tax, suspended in certain areas, revoked on occasion, and often wrongfully imposed, the *péage corporel* was the subject of many compaints and appeals to the Sovereign Council until its abolition for the entire kingdom in 1784. Many of these proceedings, and Colbert's Ordinance of 1663, regulating tariffs and tolls for Alsace, including the *péage corporel*, appear in *Recueil des édits, déclarations, lettres patentes, arrêts du conseil d'état et du conseil souverain d'Alsace, ordonnances et règlemens concernant cette province*, edited by M. de Boug (Colmar, 1775). Volume 1, covering the years 1657 to 1725, reproduces with additions an earlier *Recueil des ordonnances d'Alsace*, edited by Nicolas de Corberon, fils (Colmar, 1738). Volume 2 of the de Boug edition covers the years 1726-1770; the collection will be cited hereafter as *Ordonnances d'Alsace*.
24 Gérard to d'Ormesson, Paris, September 23, 1783, AA 2658, fol. 55-62; Gérard to d'Ormesson, to Ségur, to Vergennes, all on October 17, 1783, from Paris, AA 2658, fol. 68-71; again to Vergennes, October 17, 1783, AA 2658, fol. 72. Gérard to the Garde des Sceaux, to the maréchal de Ségur, to the Contrôleur-Général, Fontainebleau, October 23, 1783, AA 2658, fol. 74-75. Gérard to Ségur, Strasbourg, February 8, 1784, AA 2658, fol. 90-92.
25 Gérard to Ségur, Paris, July 11, 1783, AA 2658, fol. 34-36; Gérard to Calonne, Paris, December 19, 1783, AA 2658, fol. 82-83.
26 Gérard to M. de Villedeuil, Paris, May 28, 1784, AA 2658, fol. 113.

Alsace, being made up neither of elections nor other royal jurisdictions, its oldtime division into departmental bailiwicks will be preserved."[27] Accordingly, bailiwicks were joined in groups of eight, nine, or ten to create three districts for Upper Alsace and three for Lower Alsace; these were later paired, and used as the electoral basis for the Estates. The significance of the arrangement lay in the fact that the bailiwicks encompassed without exception all Alsatian territories. Thus the possessions of the foreign princes, like those of French landholders, would become subject to the taxes which it was the first business of the district assemblies, meeting by orders, to establish and allocate.[28]

As the time drew near for choosing deputies to the district assemblies, the members of the clerical chapter of Neuviller decided to prepare themselves for the task by seeking information on the "principal objects which could interest not only the clergy, but also the province and the whole nation," in the district assembly, in the next provincial estates, and the Estates-General as well.[29] It was quite an order. The chapter's patriotic zeal and eagerness to distinguish themselves before their colleagues may seem naïve today, but not in 1789, in the prevailing atmosphere of enthusiasm for reform. A set of guidelines prepared in response to the Chapter's request was pirated and published anonymously as a public service by a zealous editor.[30] Both internal and external evidence point to Conrad-Alexandre Gérard as author of the *Projet d'instructions pour le chapitre de . . . à l'Assemblée du District* (hereafter referred to as the *Projet*), an urgent plea for reform which constitutes in a sense a *cahier de doléances* for the province of Alsace.

When the pamphlet was filed in the Bibliothèque Universitaire et Nationale of Strasbourg, the name Gérard was written in brackets on the title page. Comparison of the text with the writings of the last *préteur* seems to demonstrate that he and not some other Gérard (a common name) was the author. Listing of the abuses plaguing Alsace echoes many of the concerns voiced in Gérard's correspondence with the court, and extensive knowledge of the institutions, customs, and laws of the province show the *Projet* to be the work of an administrator experienced in Alsatian affairs. The date of composition was early 1789, in the interval between the electoral ordinance for the Estates, issued January 29, and the elections themselves, which took place in February and March. Gérard was in Paris all or part of that time, said to be in poor health,[31] although the pamphlet and several vigorous letters

27 *Procès-verbal des séances de l'assemblée provinciale d'Alsace tenue à Strasbourg aux mois de novembre et décembre 1787* (Strasbourg, 1788), pp. 25, 26.
28 Reuss, *Histoire d'Alsace*, p. 197.
29 [Gérard], *Projet d'instructions*, p. 5.
30 So says the editor in his preface, claiming that he published the work as a public service; the explanation may have been a smoke screen to protect the author's anonymity.
31 Allegations of poor health and absence from Strasbourg at a critical time were made

of this period could scarcely have come from the pen of a man who was seriously ill. Editor and author admit that the work was done in haste; with the deadline of the elections to meet, there would have been no time for research, and only a writer with a thorough mastery of his subject could have given it such detailed and knowledgeable treatment. What clinches the matter of authorship is mention of certain provisions of the voting laws of the United States and the proceedings of the Notables obtainable only at first hand. Although no documentary evidence has been found linking Gérard with the chapter of Neuviller, there can be no doubt that he wrote the *Projet*.

The basic concepts expressed in the work show the influence of a lifelong preoccupation with the law of nations and of Rome. In the language of the *Projet*, French men and women are not subjects, they are citizens, born with certain inalienable rights, and a mandate to exercise their will through their own representatives. A fundamental principle to be established in all of France, in the provincial estates as well as in the general, is a concept of organic law: the right of self-taxation. Every Frenchman, every free man and citizen has possessed this right from time immemorial, as shown by the *don volontaire* of the clergy, and the *don gratuit* of the *pays d'état*.[32] Throughout centuries of despotism, these voluntary offerings have borne witness to the "unwritten principle of public law which proscribes any impost not granted by the nation."[33] Once this postulate is conceded, the abuses of the past may be corrected. Many of these originated with the special status of Alsace, which must be dissolved, and a more perfect union formed with France—not with the present tyrannous and corrupt regime, but with a kingdom purged and regenerated by reform.[34] The supreme objective of the deputies of Alsace in the Estates must be to amalgamate her own constitution with that of the entire kingdom so effectively that "every Alsatian may say: *there are no more Voges* [sic] with as much satisfaction as Louis XIV said to his grandson: *there are no more Pyrenees.*"[35]

First and foremost among "the grievances which overwhelm us" is financial privilege. Gérard's list of injustices caused by exemptions and special treatment is long. Among the worst abuses are taxes by mini-

by Frédéric de Dietrich (see note 57) who replaced Gérard in the functions of *préteur* in July, 1789. Gabriel G. Ramon, *Frédéric de Dietrich, Premier Maire de Strasbourg sous la Révolution* (Paris and Strasbourg, 1919), makes frequent references to the "ailing Gérard."

32 [Gérard], *Projet d'instructions*, p. 54.
33 Ibid.
34 Ibid., pp. 33-34. "At this moment the dawn of a beautiful day is shining over France; . . . we cherish the hope of having the wisest administration, the most just, the most favorable to her citizens. . . ." Ford, *Strasbourg in Transition*, p. 234, remarks that "by Louis XVI's time few Strasburgers seem to have considered being subjects of any one but the King of France."
35 [Gérard], *Projet d'instructions*, p. 8. John B. Wolf, *Louis XIV* (New York, 1968), p. 507, ascribes the speech about the Pyrenees not to Louis XIV, but to the Spanish ambassador.

sterial decree, continued collection of special levies after their purpose
has been achieved, the tax to support the militia which is onerous to the
poor, the quartering of military personnel upon civilians, payment of
pensions for the interior out of taxes levied in Alsace,[36] exemption of
the clergy and *noblesse* from taxes for public works and roads, and the
corresponding personal *corvée* imposed upon the Third Estate, the
devastating regime of the tax farms, especially the odious *aides* and
gabelle—all are inadmissible, all must go. "Let the very name of financial privilege be destroyed,"[37] and with it the exemption of foreign
princes. They pay no taxes in Alsace, yet they collect feudal dues, and
claim representation in the provincial estates! Suppose their claims to
be allowed, all of the following might attend:

> The bishops of Strasbourg, of Spire and of Basel, the chapters of Stras-
> bourg, Guebwiller and of Wissembourg, the abbey of Munster, the
> princes of Hesse, of Deux-Ponts, Baden and Würtemburg, Broglie and
> Linange; the Grand Prefect, the lords of Oberbronne, the Duke of Valen-
> tinois, the Immediate Nobility, etc. etc., all would have the right to sit
> personally or send their representatives to our provincial estates inde-
> pendently of any mandate.[38]

French born and French naturalized citizens alone have the right to sit
in our provincial estates. The common interest requires that "trust and
a free choice confer, to the exclusion of birth, wealth, and powers
[*dignités*] the right to decide the fate of all."[39]

Likewise, the demands of the *féodalité*, which "can only lead to the
establishment of a dangerous aristocracy," must be repudiated;[40] not so
the division of society into orders, which is fundamental to the constitution of France, originating with Charlemagne.[41] The orders are as old
as the nation; the nation alone can change them. They are essential to
the preservation of an "enlightened liberty," which will find its political
solutions in a *juste milieu*, somewhere between the "petulant impatience" which overturns and destroys and the "apathy which is the fruit
of despotism."[42] Presumably there will be greater equality in the future
relationship among the orders, for the Third Estate will not aspire to
rise from the role of oppressed merely to assume that of oppressor.
This and other great issues will be decided by the Estates-General only;
it is they who will establish the definitive relationship among the

---

36 Here one suspects a personal grievance. Gérard's salary (*traitement*) as *préteur* was
    "burdened with two pensions of 3000 livres each, for the benefit of two ladies, each
    one younger" than he. His protests against this drain on his resources were of no
    avail. Gérard to (?), Versailles, April 14, 1781, AA 2657, no. 1; Gérard to Joly de
    Fleury, Strasbourg, July 1, 1781, AA 2657, no. 19.
37 [Gérard], *Projet d'instructions*, p. 40.
38 Ibid., p. 33. He disapproved the claims of Strasbourg and of the Decapole to special
    representation in the Estates, which Necker granted, notwithstanding.
39 Ibid., p. 26.
40 Ibid.
41 Ibid., pp. 6, 56.
42 Ibid., p. 34.

orders, determine which subjects are properly the concern of each, and on what occasions they deliberate in common, how far resistance may go, etc.[43]

In the realm of justice,[44] Gérard denounces arbitrary arrest in any form, and upholds the right of the citizen to be tried before the civil authorities alone. He recommends abolition of the tribunal of the military police (*maréchaussée*) and sees the necessity of shielding the judges in manorial courts from the "caprice" of the seigneurs, who threaten their independence; he suggests reforms in accounting and procedure, and the establishment of a third court to hear petty claims and speed the wheels of justice clogged by a multitude of cases. Otherwise, the courts should remain on the footing enjoyed since the reunion, for Alsatians cherish the privilege of litigation before their own tribunals. The city of Strasbourg has obtained the right of appeal to the *conseil d'état*, but this is prejudicial to parties bringing action against the city, and must be revoked. The Sovereign Council, not the *conseil d'état*, is the highest tribunal of the province. It has been charged with registering the laws passed by the provincial estates, and must remain the bulwark of the rights and privileges of the Alsatian constitution. Thus Gérard, despite his wish for a more perfect union, voices that particularism which in the National Assembly, a few months later, would resist more stoutly than privilege the "contagion" of the night of August 4.[45]

Coming at last to the clergy, at whose behest he took up his pen, Gérard analyzes their needs and proposes specific reforms which lead inevitably to the crucial one, the sacrifice of privilege. He begins with a concession, by enjoining the chapter members to take exception to number ten of the Articles of Convocation limiting representation of ecclesiastical bodies[46] on the grounds that canons and members of monastic orders have not relinquished their titles by virtue of a decision to live in common. Every member should attend, or if it proves inadvisable to move the whole order, send a proxy.

Representation of the non-beneficed clergy, on the other hand, raises a very delicate question. For them to vote as clergymen is "anticonstitutional," for the clerical order is legally composed of only two classes: those who hold title to a benefice, or those who have been admitted to sacred orders. Clearly the non-beneficed clergy are excluded, as are the ministers of the Protestant faith who, however capable and upstanding they may be, are part of the Third Estate.[47]

43 Ibid., p. 51.
44 Most of these recommendations occur on pp. 43ff. of the *Projet d'instructions*.
45 Georges Lefebvre, *The Coming of the French Revolution*, trans. by R. R. Palmer (Princeton, 1947), p. 165.
46 In the bailiwick assembly of the clergy, the holders of a benefice, whether bishopric, priory, abbey, or parish were limited to a single representative only. Cf. Lefebvre, *Coming of the French Revolution*, p. 55.
47 [Gérard], *Projet d'instructions*, p. 30.

It is to the interest of the entire order to improve the lot of its humbler members. The revenues of the royal curés in Alsace should be raised at least to the level of those on the *portion congrue*,[48] for the former are often assigned to the poorest parishes where they can scarcely maintain themselves, let alone assist the needy. Those on the *portion congrue* are not much better off, being constantly penalized by rising costs and inflation. Their income could be increased by diverting to them the revenues of the *bénéfice simple* as the titularies die off, for the *bénéfice simple* is a sinecure, requiring neither residence nor service, and should be abolished. Inequalities in future taxation must be avoided by imposing higher taxes on large benefices and on non-resident beneficiaries. The apportionment of taxes may be made by the diocesan chambers, but under no circumstances should they have a voice in the decision-making process. The true representatives of the clergy are the deputies whom they will send to the Estates. They are the ones who will decide to tax themselves and all members of their order, it is they who will turn over to the state the revenues of their foundations. In so doing, they need not fear contravention of the pious intent of the donors, for charity is the first duty of the state, and the state encompasses all society, poor and rich alike.[49]

Thus the chapter of Neuviller has been led step by step to the heart of Gérard's message: the renunciation of privilege. He makes a stirring appeal:

> The moment of sacrifice has come; the misery of the people, disorder in the finances, excessive and ruinous taxes, an enormous public debt, the reestablishment of credit, all demand it of the citizens; when an edifice is about to crumble, is there a hand which will withstay the impulse to shore it up?[50]

But there must be safeguards. The clergy's "generous relinquishment of its rights and privileges" will be made to the nation assembled in its three orders, and only on the following conditions: that there be no taxation without consent of the Estates; that *lettres de cachet* be abolished, and every citizen guaranteed the right to a fair trial; that the

48 The benefice provided income from land, rents, etc. so that the vicars and curés could devote their time to the care (*cure*) of the souls entrusted to them. In default of income from rent or lands, the *portion congrue* was a cost of living benefice which necessarily diminished with the passage of time and the rise in prices. Augmentation of the *portion congrue* was proposed by the Assembly of the Clergy in 1760 and again in 1765. An edict of May, 1768 fixed the equivalent in money of a living at £1500. For purposes of comparison, it may be noted that yearly salaries of teachers in the colleges of Strasbourg, Colmar, and Molsheim, reorganized in the mid-sixties after the expulsion of the Jesuits, were as follows: teachers of the lower grades (classes 6-3) received £500 or £600; teachers of the top two classes received £700 or £800 and the administrators, sub-principal and principal, £800 and £1000, respectively. *Lettres patentes* regulating the colleges of Strasbourg, of Colmar, and of Molsheim in 1765, de Boug (ed.), *Ordonnances d'Alsace*, 2: 703-708.
49 [Gérard], *Projet d'instructions*, pp. 56, 57.
50 Ibid., p. 52.

interval between meetings of the Estates never exceed five years.[51] When these "imprescriptible rights" have become part of the "fundamental laws of the monarchy,"[52] then, and only then, will the clergy sacrifice its privileges, and freed of the hatred and jealousy which these have inspired, lead the nation to reform.

Gérard's insistence on the abolition of privilege places him squarely in the ranks of those demanding sweeping change, especially on the part of the Third Estate. But he places himself in conflict with them by his reverence for the "constitution of Charlemagne," and the division of society into orders, wherein he reflects the viewpoint of the government bureaucracy for whom the greatest crimes were lèse-Majesté and innovation against the constitution. In denouncing the privileges which set apart the first two orders, he robs them of their base of support, and his program appears in the light of an unworkable compromise. That the attempt to solve the nation's problems might lead to cataclysm, he perceived: "In the present state of affairs we can anticipate either the regeneration or the dissolution of the kingdom into all its component parts."[53] He closes his instructions to the clergy with an appeal to exhibit the utmost generosity, calm, and restraint in order to stave off the twin scourges of intrigue and violence.

His hope was not to be fulfilled. Whether the Projet served "at least a momentary usefulness" in the education of the public or whether it incurred rapid oblivion along with so many others,[54] the lull before the storm in Alsace was soon to end. Violence came on the heels of privation.[55] A poor grain harvest in 1787, followed a year later by a winter of bitter cold, brought the price of bread to famine level in the spring of 1789. The Magistracy was accused of indifference, and the dismissal of Necker caused demonstrations in July. With the arrival on the eighteenth of the special courier bringing news of the fall of the Bastille, unrest and disorder turned into riot. On July 21, some of the magistrates were forced to flee their homes in terror, while a crowd ransacked the Hôtel de Ville, pillaging the cash drawers and the wine cellar, throwing papers out of the windows, destroying records, furnishings, everything that came their way, and, as in the engravings "Plünderung des Rathauses,"[56] throwing tiles and plaster from the roof.

51 Ibid., p. 58.
52 Ibid., pp. 57, 58.
53 Ibid., p. 20.
54 Ibid., pp. 2, 3, Editor's Notice.
55 H. Brunschwig, "Les Débuts de la Révolution à Strasbourg," La Vie en Alsace (1928), p. 119: "There is no history of the Revolution in Strasbourg before the year 1790. But there is the history of the great economic crises of 1789-90."
56 Johann Hans (fl. 1800), Strasbourg-born painter and copper engraver, did a series of scenes of the Strasbourg of his day, including a painting of the sack of the Hôtel de Ville which served as inspiration for a celebrated engraving of the same subject by J.-M. Weis, II (note 16). His engraving and another by N. Devere were reproduced

Gérard was not in Strasbourg at that time, but in Paris; his ill health
had served as a pretext for his replacement by a younger man, an
ambitious aspirant to the title and emoluments of *préteur*, Frédéric de
Dietrich.[57] Being a Lutheran, Dietrich could not hope to have his
nomination ratified by the Sovereign Council, so he settled for the
designation of "King's commissioner with the functions of *préteur*," in
which capacity he was installed just fifteen days before the sack of the
Hôtel de Ville.

Arthur Young was in Strasbourg on that memorable day, a witness
to the pillaging, and so was Rochambeau, newly arrived as provincial
commander. Their descriptions are part of the vivid testimony which
has survived, including letters, newspaper accounts, depositions, etc.
After minute reviewing of the sources, and restoration step by step of
the events, a great Alsatian scholar verified the opinion of earlier
writers that the sack of the Hôtel de Ville was the result of direction and
planning.[58]

But whose? Reuss does not say. One by one he examines and
discards the villains tossed up in the storm of accusations which lasted
over a century. It was not the central government, it was not the
intendant, nor the strangely indecisive Rochambeau; it was not the
bourgeoisie, nor the Catholics, nor indeed, the Lutherans. It was not
the King's commissioner, Dietrich, whose death on the scaffold four
years later would lay his previous conduct open to suspicion and to
doubt.

There was only one man of importance left whose decision, or
want of it, could have affected the course of the riot that day. This was
Baron de Klinglin, grandson of the accused *préteur*, and leader of the
militia of Strasbourg. Subsequently it became known that during the
confusion all the documents relating to the malfeasance of his grandfather had disappeared, whereupon the Baron's detractors cried "conspiracy!" But scholars have found no real evidence of guilty conduct
during the riot; they consider other aspects of the Baron's behavior
and his emigration to be more powerful indictments than his equivocal
handling of the militia.

Not all the records hurled from the windows of the Hôtel de Ville
were lost to posterity. From Paris, Gérard wrote the Magistracy offer-

by Adolph Seyboth, *Das Alte Strassburg vom 13. Jahrhundert bis zum Jahre 1870* (Strasbourg, 1890), plate 17, p. 131.
57 Frédéric de Dietrich (1748-1793) belonged to the Magistracy who, he maintained,
did not have confidence in Gérard. Dietrich, a mineralogist of repute, was elected a
member of the Academy of Sciences in 1784. His career as mayor of Strasbourg
during the Revolution was understandably stormy, but his biographer and others
believe to be unfounded the accusation of treason which brought him to the scaffold.
58 Rodolphe Reuss, "Le sac de l'Hôtel de Ville de Strasbourg," *Revue historique*, 120
(1915), 26-55, 289-322, finds no wholly satisfactory explanation for the sack of the
Hôtel de Ville. His attack on the problem has been characterized by Ford, *Strasbourg
in Transition*, p. 304, note 21, as "the most determined effort to solve the basically
insoluble problem of individual roles in the causation of the riot."

ing to have his secretary furnish copies of missing documents from his own voluminous files of the Hôtel du Préteur.[59] This was in December, 1789. His health was failing fast. He would not live to know whether the "more perfect union" of the beloved province with the kingdom would make his dream come true, so that every Alsatian might say, "there are no more Vosges." He did live long enough to see the end of the five-hundred-year-old Republic of Strasbourg, with Dietrich's election as Mayor on February 5, 1790. When Gérard died six weeks later (April 16), the Revolution was under way in Alsace.

59 Rodolphe Reuss, Lettre de M. Gérard, ancien Préteur, au Magistrat de Strasbourg, Paris, December 10, 1789, *Revue d'Alsace* (1880), p. 236.

Marriage, Divorce, and the Status of Women During the Terror

THEMISTOCLES RODIS

This essay seeks to present a limited but important perspective on the conflict between the ideals and the practices of the French regarding marriage and divorce during the Revolution, particularly as seen in the legislation of the Terror. Because of the frequent rhetoric used by contending groups, which so often carried moral implications, those implications must be seriously considered. The author has no intention of either avoiding or inviting the usually unresolved challenge that accompanies the consideration of this subject, namely, whether morals are universal or relative. Nor does he believe it sensible to present a value-laden definition of the term. "Morals" in this essay is used within the broadest historical interpretation and connotation of the eighteenth-century term, *moeurs*.[1] Morals, or *moeurs*, will thus be considered to encompass the ordinary conduct, behavior, and action of the French regarding marriage and divorce during the Terror and especially as effected and reflected in the legislation of that time.

During the eighteenth century, especially on the eve of the Revolution, traditional French morals appeared to have reached a low ebb. Such eminent *philosophes* and Rationalists as Montesquieu, Voltaire, Diderot, and Rousseau attacked the Old Regime at both its intellectual and institutional foundations for being an outmoded survival of medieval asceticism, for retaining an untenable religious doctrine which required "good works" for personal salvation, and for encouraging an unrealistic social grouping of the Three Estates that was based on birth rather than on ability.[2]

1 Bernard Faÿ, *The Revolutionary Spirit in France and America at the End of the Eighteenth Century*, trans. Ramon Guthrie (New York: Harcourt, Brace and Co., 1927), p. 46 and n. Cf. Arthur M. Wilson, *Diderot: The Testing Years, 1713-1759* (New York: Oxford University Press, 1957), pp. 53-54. Wilson underlines this definition of *moeurs* in his perceptive discussion of François-Vincent Toussaint's *Les Moeurs*, which he declares to be "one of the first [1748] and therefore one of the boldest works in the eighteenth century to set forth the arguments for a natural morality unbolstered by any religious arguments or public cult."

2 The following treat this subject at some length: Preserved Smith, *The History of Modern Culture* (New York, 1934), II, 596-615, 601-608; Daniel Mornet, *French Thought in the Eighteenth Century*, trans. Lawrence M. Levin (New York, 1929), pp. 128-280; Charles Louis de Secondat, Baron de la Brède et de Montesquieu,

The *philosophes* called for a new set of institutions, a different intellectual doctrine, and a revision of the social order based on Nature and Reason in order to bring about liberty, equality, individualism, and humanitarianism. Among the sincere proponents of these goals were also many opportunists who vaguely referred to these ideals as an excuse for an irresponsible hedonism.[3] Especially in the celebrated— and often notorious—salons in France, which the higher clergy and the nobility frequented and where the more ambitious bourgeoisie sought acceptability, gambling and cheating, often leading to duels or suicide, were persistent. Dancing, card playing, and theatre-going, which the clergy particularly condemned as the "engines of Satan," were widespread. Even the most scandalous happenings—marital promiscuity, adultery, and prostitution—were socially condoned while officially condemned.[4]

The bourgeoisie was caught in a dilemma at this time. On the one hand, reinforced by its own secular ethic, it attempted to live up to the high morality that the Old Regime demanded, at least formally; on the other hand, it was simultaneously attracted to and inspired by the new ideas of the *philosophes*. This dichotomy was further emphasized by the bourgeoisie's realization that by being included in the Third Estate, they were socially unacceptable to the First and Second Estates and were often politically impotent as well. At the same time, because they were generally wealthier than the first two Estates and very often intellectually superior to them, many of the bourgeoisie were resented by the rest of the Third Estate. Thus, it was the bourgeoisie, frequently represented by the *philosophes*, who became the leading critics of the morality of the higher clergy and nobility during the Old Regime and who, for the most part—as is well known—ultimately became leaders in the French Revolution when it came.[5]

Some historians of the French Revolution, for example, Carlyle[6] and Taine, generally agree that, despite the debasement of the Old Regime, morals in general became even worse after 1789. Taine found

Persian and Chinese Letters, trans. John Davidson and Oliver Goldsmith (Washington and London, 1910); idem, *Spirit of the Laws*, trans. from the French (London, 1900), vols. 1 and 2, and *Cahiers, 1716-1755*, ed. Bernard Grasset and André Masson (Paris, 1951); François Marie Arouet de Voltaire, *A Philosophical Dictionary*, ed. and trans. William F. Fleming (London and New York, 1901), vols. 1-10; Denis Diderot, *Oeuvres complètes*, ed. Jules Assézat and Maurice Tourneux (Paris, 1875-1877), vols. 1-20; Jean Baptiste Rousseau, *Oeuvres complètes*, 2d ed. (Paris, 1826), vols. 1-25, passim; also his *Correspondance général*, ed. Théophile Dufour (Paris, 1924-1934), vols. 1-20, passim.

3 Geoffrey Gorer, *The Life and Ideas of the Marquis de Sade*, 2nd ed. (London, 1953), p. 47. See also Siméon-Prosper Hardy, *Mes Loisirs: Journal des événemens . . . 1764- 1789*, ed. M. Tourneaux and M. Vitrac (Paris, 1912), I, 90, 94, 103, 360.

4 Smith, *Modern Culture*, II, 598-604.

5 Louis R. Gottschalk, *The Era of the French Revolution, 1715-1815* (Boston, 1929), pp. 42-60.

6 Thomas Carlyle, *The French Revolution, A History*, ed. J. Holland Rose, 3 vols. (London, 1902), passim.

that morals, already low in the eighteenth century, declined further after 1789.[7] In his history, *The French Revolution*, he concentrated almost entirely on "evil men and the crimes and follies they commit."[8] Taine's view of the Revolution was simply expressed in the terse statement: "It is not a revolution, but a dissolution."[9]

Other historians, such as Aulard, Mathiez, and Lefebvre disagree, arguing that the French Revolution reflected an actual improvement of morals. Aulard argued that during the Revolution morals generally improved over those of the eighteenth century because the Monarchy, the feudal system, and the state church had been abolished and an egalitarian system had replaced them.[10] Similarly, Mathiez, while admitting that morals were low during the Revolution, carefully explained that this was a result of the resistance by monarchists and bourgeoisie and the added threat of imminent foreign attack.[11] Finally, Lefebvre, although taking essentially a middle position, nevertheless contended that morals improved because "state intervention [maintained] justice among the social classes."[12]

It can be demonstrated that most of these opinions of morals during the French Revolution were derivative explanations and could, therefore, be evaluated only on a *post-hoc* basis.[13] The purpose of this essay is to present the ideals, aims, and practices of the French revolutionists during the Terror and to determine in what ways legislation on marriage and divorce—proposed, debated, or passed— affected or reflected the morals of the French peole.

It is widely accepted that Montesquieu, Voltaire, Diderot, and Rousseau were the four *philosophes* whose ideals and precepts of morality had the greatest popularity among the leaders of the French Revolution.[14] But the one most frequently mentioned, of course, is Rousseau.[15] The ideals which the *philosophes* propounded and to which the

7 Hippolyte A. Taine, *The Ancient Regime*, trans. John Durand (New ed. rev.; New York, 1896), pp. v-x.

8 George P. Gooch, *History and Historians in the Nineteenth Century* (New York and London, 1928), p. 243.

9 Hippolyte A. Taine, *The French Revolution*, trans. John Durand, 3 vols. (New York, 1897), I, 1.

10 François V. A. Aulard, *Histoire politique de la Révolution française . . . 1789-1804* (Paris, 1901). See also the only official English translation, but which has been badly received: *The French Revolution: A Political History, 1789-1804*, trans. from the 3rd ed., Bernard Miall (New York, 1910), vols. 1-4. The books that demonstrate Aulard's conclusions most clearly are *La Révolution française et les congrégations* (Paris, 1903), and *La Révolution française et la régime féodale* (Paris, 1919).

11 Albert Mathiez, *The French Revolution*, trans. Catherine Allison Phillips (New York, 1928).

12 Georges Lefebvre, *Etudes sur la Révolution française* (Paris, 1954). Here Lefebvre's views are clearly presented in essays on the political, economic, agrarian, and social history of the French Revolution.

13 Carl L. Becker, *Everyman His Own Historian* (New York, 1935).

14 Daniel Mornet, *Les Origines intellectuelles de la Révolution française, 1715-1787*, 2d ed. (Paris, 1934), pp. 89-92.

15 Beatrice F. Hyslop, *A Guide to the General Cahiers of 1789* (New York, 1936), p. 75,

revolutionists became committed, as is well known, were the concept of natural rights (which included the ideals of liberty, equality, fraternity, and humanitarianism) and the ambiguous concept of the social contract which involved the State, the individual's relationship to it, and its paradoxical consequences.[16] While there appeared to be general accord among the *philosophes* on the former, there was almost no agreement concerning the latter by either the *philosophes* or the French revolutionsts—especially during the Terror.

In the attempt by the revolutionists to put these ideals into practice, three major areas of conflict emerged. First there was the struggle between the intellectual and religious premises of the Old Regime, based upon the Christian doctrine of personal salvation through "good works," on the one hand, and the assumption of the *philosophes* and revolutionists of secular humanitarianism on the other, which was based on the operation of Nature and Reason.[17] (The *philosophes* were especially critical of the Church's inclusion of the taking of the sacraments as "good works" in and of themselves.) Second, there was the contradiction between the *philosophes'* ideals and the attempts by the revolutionists to apply them realistically to the practical problems of the Revolution. Finally, there was the discrepancy between the basic agreement among revolutionists on the eighteenth-century principles of Nature and Reason and the actual, often agonizing, disagreement on their interpretation, meaning, application, and even their relevance.[18] This last conflict seems to have been the most frustrating to the revolutionists themselves as well as to their friends and supporters abroad, as is evident in the works of Sir James Mackintosh, Arthur Young, and William Wordsworth.[19]

n. 123. See also Claude G. Bowers, *Pierre Vergniaud, Voice of the French Revolution* (New York, 1950); H. Morse Stephens (ed.), *The Principal Speeches of the Statesmen and Orators of the French Revolution, 1789-1795*, 2 vols. (Oxford, 1892), I, 100, 251, 454; II, 21, 294, 296, 297, 323, 402, 406. M. Theuret, "Analyse des idées principales" (1789), in *French Revolution Pamphlets at Western Reserve University*, III, 1, 3, 5.

16 Henri Peyre, "The Influence of Eighteenth Century Ideas on the French Revolution," *Journal of the History of Ideas* 10 (January 1949), 63-87, and "Rapport de Hentz . . . de Cambacérès, 1793 . . ."; Philippe Sagnac, *Législation civile de la Révolution française . . . (1794-1804)* (Paris, 1889), p. 43.

17 F. J. C. Hearnshaw (ed.), *Social and Political Ideas of Some Great Thinkers of the Age of Reason* (London, 1930).

18 Crane Brinton, *A Decade of Revolution, 1789-1799* (New York, 1934), pp. 117-63.

19 Sir James Mackintosh, *Vindiciae Gallicae: Defence of the French Revolution and its English Admirers*, 4th ed. (London, 1792), pp. 105-109, 113, 115-22, 174-76, 216-18, 263-64, 306-308, 323-24, 337-38. It was published as a direct reply to Burke's *Reflections*. Cf. Alfred Cobban (ed.), *The Debate on the French Revolution, 1789-1800* (London, 1950), p. 92. Even Mackintosh (although it took him longer than most), by 1801 "was anxious to 'wipe off the disgrace of having been once betrayed into an approbation of that conspiracy against God and Man,' the French revolution." See also Arthur Young, *Travels in France . . .* , ed. M. Betham-Edwards (London, 1906), pp. 155-56. Writing on June 11, 1789, Young expressed hope and even enthusiasm for the peaceful success of the Revolution; cf. ibid., pp. 322-24, 340-41. But by April of 1793, he found it "impossible to justify the excesses of the [French] people on their taking up arms. . . ." See also William Wordsworth, "Prelude," Book X, p. 407, lines 105-44,

A first step on the road to accomplishing the revolutionists' goals was that of secularizing the social institutions. Although the Monarchy during the Old Regime had already taken some steps in this direction, marriage and divorce (as well as illegitimacy) continued to be considered the almost exclusive province of the Roman Catholic Church. Over the strenuous objections of the *philosophes*, the Church had managed successfully to maintain marriage as part of the sacramental system; moreover, it accepted illegitimacy as a subject for Christian charity under the doctrine of "good works." Both were related to the question of personal salvation; but, in any case, women were held more accountable than men in these matters.[20]

Taking their cue from the *philosophes*, the revolutionists decided that these matters were to be equalized and secularized under the two eighteenth-century doctrines, natural rights and the social contract. In questions of marriage and divorce, therefore, all individuals were to be equal; furthermore, these issues were to be the legal responsibility of the State, not of the Church. The Church, it followed, was to subordinate itself accordingly. The inclusion in the Constitution of 1791 of the remarkable statement that "Marriage, under the law, shall be considered only as a civil contract"[21] was the major formal and legal step to secularization. This declaration is all the more surprising in view of the fact that only one-third of the *cahiers* had asked for any degree of secularization of the register, and not one had called specifically for the secularization of marriage itself.[22] Yet, within one year, the decree of September 20, 1792 formally secularized marriage and divorce, confirmed the steps already taken for the subordination of the Church to the State, and gave women legal equality with men.[23]

These conflicts between eighteenth-century ideals and revolutionary practices culminated in the decree of 12 Brumaire, Year II, in which the National Convention gave illegitimate children equal status

in Ernest de Selincourt, ed., *The Prelude: or Growth of a Poet's Mind*, 2nd ed., rev., Helen Darbishire (Oxford, Clarendon Press, 1959). Wordsworth enthusiastically described the Revolution in 1792 between the opening line (105), "O Pleasant exercise of hope and joy!" and the closing lines (143-44), ". . . the place, where, in the end, / We find our happiness, or not at all!" Cf. "Prelude," book XI, p. 412, lines 206-208. But by 1799 at the time of the French invasion of Switzerland, Wordsworth was accusing Frenchmen:

> But now, become oppressors in their turn,
> Frenchmen had changed a war of self-defence
> For one of conquest, losing sight of all. . . .

20 Jacques Godechot, *Les Institutions de la France sous la Révolution et l'Empire* (Paris, 1951), pp. 204-207, 216-21.
21 "Constitution of 3 September 1791" (Title II, Article 7), in *Select Documents Illustrative of the History of the French Revolution*, ed. Leopold G. Wickham (Oxford, 1905), II, 220.
22 Beatrice F. Hyslop, *French Nationalism in 1789 According to the General Cahiers* (New York, 1934), pp. 8, 107, 199.
23 "Decree determining the Recording of Vital Statistics," in John Hall Stewart, *A Documentary Survey of the French Revolution* (New York, 1951), pp. 322-40.

in *all* matters with legitimate children.[24] The ideal of equality in this instance clashed with the ideal of individualism, and both clashed directly with the practices of property rights and inheritance. The inability of the revolutionists to resolve such conflicts effectively resulted in the ultimate nullificaton of the decree, in practice, by the courts, the ministers of justice, and Cambacérès' committee as early as 1795.[25]

These conflicts among revolutionists—whether or not to accept the principles of the *philosophes*—and the disparity between their interpretations and applications are probably best revealed in the legislation that was passed between 1789 and 1795 concerning marriage, divorce, and illegitimacy. Between 1789 and 1792, laws favoring the individual were passed frequently and with comparatively little opposition. After 1792, and particularly in 1793, when the legislators were continuing to proclaim essentially the same ideals as before, their proposed legislation favoring the individual was almost regularly defeated. Decrees which made the State supreme, however, were regularly passed with little or no opposition during the whole of this period. Attitudes toward marriage, divorce, and illegitimacy, therefore, reflected the basic conflicts inherent in the issue of individualism versus *étatism* and between the concept of natural rights as opposed to public welfare (humanitarianism). Furthermore, in all three areas there occurred numerous conflicts over interpretation of concepts even when there was agreement in principle.[26]

It should be noted that although there was a general acceptance of the principle of the equal rights of men (albeit, not necessarily of women) there continued to exist throughout the Revolution a strong and persistent minority who remained united in their unfailing opposition to any change in the traditional morals. These defenders of the Old Regime not only continued to argue that individuals were inherently unequal, but they also introduced new arguments to justify their contention, even utilizing the doctrine of natural rights. According to them, sex, nationality, social position, religion, and even the professions were justifiable legal inequalities. Furthermore, they argued that in practice (whatever the theory) individuals were in fact distinguished from one another by wealth, custom, and law.[27]

24 Crane Brinton, *French Revolutionary Legislation on Illegitimacy, 1789-1804* (Cambridge, Massachusetts, 1938), passim.
25 Ibid., pp. 42, 72.
26 Sagnac, *Législation civile*, pp. 381-99.
27 Paul Beik, *The French Revolution Seen From the Right: Social Theories in Motion, 1789-1799* (Philadelphia, 1956), pp. 1, 3-13. Two such examples given by Beik are Jacob Nicolas Moreau, "a faithful servant of absolutism," and Louis le Laurai, Comte d'Antraigues, "an extremist among the aristocrats." Moreau in fact continued to advocate the traditional arguments to their logical extremity even in the midst of the French Revolution itself. The Comte d'Antraigues was as ardent a follower of Rousseau as was Robespierre himself (but from the opposite viewpoint) and actually

The difficulties faced by revolutionists in their attempt to secularize marriage and divorce may, perhaps, be understood more clearly in retrospect by recalling that even after the Revolution and, specifically, since the time of Napoleon, marriage in France has been considered to be the "legitimate union of a man and a woman—an institution [which is] at the same time [both] civil and religious."[28] The original question—whether the new civil authority ever replaced the old ecclesiastical establishment, in practice—is still a matter of debate in France. Nevertheless, at that time, the legislative body did its best to give predominance to the secular authorities by decreeing that the municipalities receive, register, administer, and maintain all records pertaining to births, marriages, and deaths.[29]

Yet, less than a year later, on November 17, 1793, this same Convention experienced a radical change of heart as it cast a disillusioned eye upon its former, almost lyrical, expression of natural rights which had included equal status for women.[30] One of the first to express this change in attitude was Chaumette, procurator of the Paris Commune.[31] Amid a chorus of approving voices, he first scolded a deputation of women for bursting unheralded into the Convention when they should have been home taking care of their children and obeying their husbands, and then moved for confirmation of his conviction that "the woman's place [is] in the home and only the man's in politics."[32] Not only was his motion unanimously accepted, but it was also decided to prohibit the deputation from speaking.

Aside from these contradictions between theory and practice, several instances of ludicrous extremes to which marriage as a civil contract was carried in the name of egalitarianism may also be cited. Helen Maria Williams, admittedly an unfriendly English witness of the Revolution, tells of a seamstress who was thrown into prison on false charges by a disgruntled suitor whose sole objective in wanting to marry her had been to get control of her business.[33] It is doubtful whether this example was imitated widely, and the abuse of revolutionary ideals for personal reasons is by no means limited to the eighteenth century; but

used the theory of natural rights to justify *inequality*: Rousseau's social contract, he argued, was formed in order that "the representatives of the general will could preserve [private] property."

28 P. A. Chéruel, *Dictionnaire historique... de la France*, 8th ed. (Paris, 1910), II, 735.
29 J. B. Duvergier, ed., *Collection complète des lois... de 1788 à 1830...* (Paris, 1834-1836), 4: 482-83; and J. Mavidal and M. E. Laurent, eds., *Archives parlementaires de 1787 à 1860...*, 1st series (Paris, 1802-1813), 55: 151. (Hereafter *Archives parlementaires.*)
30 "Séance de 27 brumaire an II," in Léonard Gallois (ed.), *Réimpression de l'ancien Moniteur... (mai 1789-novembre 1799)* Paris, 1850-1854), 18: 450. (Hereafter *Moniteur.*)
31 Ibid.
32 Ibid., 17, 574. See also Robert R. Palmer, *Twelve Who Ruled: The Committee of Public Safety During the Terror* (Princeton, 1941), pp. 46-47.
33 Helen Maria Williams, *Residence in France... 1792-95...* (London, 1906), II, 379.

that such incidents could occur at all is a commentary on the judicial process under the Terror. When the Terror was at its height, too often all that was necessary to arrest a suspect was merely an unconfirmed accusation of alleged infidelity to the Republic[34]—a procedure that could easily be turned against a personal enemy. Another example of exploiting revolutionary ideals for self-serving purposes—perhaps more comic opera than grim reality—is illustrated by an anecdote told by Mlle des Echerolles, a member of the nobility who managed to escape the guillotine during the Terror. An ignorant country bumpkin, she relates, unexpectedly presented himself for marriage to a noblewoman by attempting to "requisition" her in the so-called "free exercise of his rights."[35] Although the lady managed to escape from her predicament, not all were apparently as fortunate in avoiding "forced marriages"—a practice that was understandably condemned by the nobility. Some of these marriages resulted from efforts to save property; others came from frantic efforts to avoid suspicion of being connected with *émigrés* or former *ci-devants*.

One of the more serious problems that came to the attention of the National Convention during the Terror was that of public executions, especially of pregnant women. Married pregnant women suspected of disloyalty to the Revolution and condemned to the guillotine[36] were a serious problem involving humanitarian considerations.[37] A related problem that troubled members of the Convention undoubtedly had greater political than moral implications—although moral arguments were often invoked.[38] This had to do with the reaction of pregnant women who were often inadvertant spectators of public executions.[39]

34 *Archives parlementaires*, 74: 303-304. See also Palmer, *Twelve*, pp. 305-12; and John R. Sirich, *Revolutionary Committees in the Departments of France, 1793-94* (Cambridge, Massachusetts, 1943), passim.
35 Alexandrine des Echerolles, *Memoirs . . . of the Terror*, trans. M. Balfour (London and New York, 1904), p. 207.
36 Hyslop, *Guide*, pp. 140-41. While the *cahiers* do not at any place specifically mention the capital punishment of women, pregnant or otherwise, Hyslop makes it clear that a great many of the *cahiers* are concerned with "egalitarianism" and "humanitarianism" in all matters of punishment by the state. At least forty of the *cahiers* asked either for the abolition of capital punishment entirely, or that its use be limited to only a few of the most serious crimes.
37 Smith, *Modern Culture*, II, 588. "The rise of a new spirit of humanitarianism . . . is a phenomenon . . . [that was introduced] . . . as the most important element in the moral tone of the Enlightenment, one that deserves and repays the most thoughtful consideration." See also John Herman Randall, Jr., *The Making of the Modern Mind* (Cambridge, Massachusetts: Houghton-Mifflin, 1940), pp. 370-71. ". . . the great ideals of the Age of Enlightenment [were] *humanitarianism*, toleration, pacifisim, cosmopolitanism" (italics mine).
38 Smith, *Modern Culture*, II, 592-93. "In the secular field, Daniel Defoe was the first social reformer [humanitarian] of the modern age. [He combined] a consuming interest in the problems of poverty, unemployment, old age, and *feminism*, with a journalist's instinct for appealing to the newly aroused social-passions . . ." (italics mine).
39 John G. Alger, *Paris in 1789-94; farewell letters . . .* (London, 1902), p. 169. Alger cites the case of a pregnant Englishwoman who was condemned in October of 1793. He

Women, as is well known, often played an active role throughout the Revolution, individually and in groups,[40] something Robespierre, for one, both recognized and exploited politically.[41] Pregnant women, however, made neither ideal victims nor good spectators at public executions. Because their reaction as spectators so often aroused sympathy for the victims and brought the Revolution itself into question, a number of legislators resorted to moral arguments to solve this political embarrassment, proposing that public executions be eliminated.[42]

The humane attitude seemed to prevail in the end. Between September 1794 and April 1795 several proposals were made which seemed to carry humanitarian connotations. The Convention had earlier passed a decree "in favor of the children and widows of the victims of Champ de Mars,"[43] which coincided with another proposal to commute the death sentences of eight pregnant women "in the name of humanity,"[44] thus linking victims of the Constitutional Monarchy with those of the Republic. In April 1795, coincident with another subsequent proposal by the same deputy to prohibit the execution of all pregnant women, another decree was recommended to outlaw capital punishment for all women, regardless of their physical or mental condition.[45]

gives no source for this incident, however, nor does he indicate the final disposition of the case. See also John G. Alger, *Glimpses of the French Revolution* (New York, n.d.), p. 234. Here Alger tells of two cases, neither of which has been substantiated. In all fairness, however, it must be noted that Alger's assertion that "only eight women respited on this account [i.e., pregnancy] were in prison on September 17 [1794]" has been substantiated by at least one witness. Cf. Honoré Riouffe, "Mémoires d'un détenu" (an III), in Charles A. Dauban (ed.), *Les Prisons de Paris sous la Révolution . . .* (Paris, 1870), p. 114: "Several days before 9 Thermidor, of the [many] women dragged to their death, several had declared themselves pregnant."

40 George Rudé, *The Crowd in the French Revolution* (London, 1959), pp. 180-90. See also Stephens, *Principal Speeches*, I, 475. As late as May 20, 1795 crowds of women in action were referred to as "furies of the guillotine." See also Alger, *Glimpses*, pp. 154-55: "In 1795, the 'Megaeras' [Furies], as the Girondins had styled them, had their last innings." See also Carlyle, *French Revolution*, pp. 593-94.

41 Maximilien Robespierre, "Speeches of 18 floréal an II" (May 7, 1794), in Stephens, *Principal Speeches*, I, 414-16. One passage in this speech is particularly pertinent, where he cries out: "O femmes françaises, chérissez la liberté achetée au prix de leur sang. . . ."

42 Riouffe, "Mémoirs," in Dauban, *Prisons*, pp. 80-133; Baron Honoré Riouffe, who was himself one of those scheduled for public execution, tells of women who, although already dead (for many condemned individuals, both men and women, somehow managed to commit suicide even during their final ride to their execution), were still guillotined. Cf. P. Caron (ed.), *Paris pendant la Terreur: Rapports des agents sécrèts du ministre de l'Intérieur*, 6 vols. (Paris, 1910-1914), V, 39; 140-41; 159. Two members of the secret police, Perriéres and Latour-Lamontagne, reported the reactions of women in general and of pregnant women specifically to public executions. Their observations led them to recommend the advanced publication of at least the routes assigned to death carts so that people could avoid the sight of those pitiful spectacles. See also Alger, *Paris*, pp. 223-24.

43 *Moniteur*, 22: 161. They are referred to as the "Petitions de Champ de Mars," July 16 and 17, 1791.

44 *Moniteur*, 21: 784.

45 Ibid., 24: 208.

The latter proposal failed of being enacted but was referred to the Committee on Legislation for further study.

In the meantime, there were many instances of confusion on the part of both the people and their legislators regarding women's expected new role in marriage. Following the passage of the marriage law of 1792, Louis Mercier, deputy from the Seine-et-Oise Department, wrote: "There are no longer now any seductions since the great facilities offered to marriage and divorce have come to the rescue of every whim."[46] Descriptions of forced marriages by a number of contemporaries seem to confirm this view,[47] as do the careless mixing of the sexes in prison during the Terror.[48] At the same time, the ideas of equality and natural rights encouraged the acceptance of incongruous legislative proposals by deputies in the Constituent Assembly to promote the equalization of the rights of the sexes. For example, one interesting motion argued that since "man's happiness depends on women, women also [should have similar] rights."[49] Another proposed the abolition of dowries, with the added condition that "if the dowry could not be abolished, a means must be devised to prevent a husband from spending it recklessly."[50] In July 1790 one perennial letter-writer to the Convention proposed that "the distinction between the natural [i.e., illegitimate] mother and the legitimate mother . . . be destroyed."[51] In keeping with these ideas, a translation of Mary Wollstonecraft's book, *A Vindication of the Rights of Women*, "dedicated to the former Bishop of Autun,"[52] was published in 1792 and, apparently, became quite popular. In active support of these ideals, at least three clubs were organized: La Société fraternelle des deux sexes, La Société des femmes, and La Société philanthropique et patriotique de bienfaisance et des bonnes moeurs.[53]

Throughout the Revolution, but especially in 1793, women were active in expressing their opinions overtly. Immediately following the February soap riots many feminine participants were arrested. September saw them particularly active, although they were motivated more by hunger than by politics or moral considerations. One observer recorded that in the Faubourg St. Antoine "they marched around shouting, 'If our husbands made the Revolution, we shall make the counter revolution, if necessary!'"[54] The Republican Women's Club,

---

46 Louis S. Mercier, *The Picture of Paris, Before and After the Revolution* (New York, 1929), p. 250.
47 Des Echerolles, *Memoirs*, p. 215.
48 Williams, *Residence*, I, 379-81, 399.
49 *Moniteur*, 2: 262-63.
50 Ibid.
51 Ibid., 5: 20.
52 Ibid., 14: 28.
53 Ibid., 15: 435; 17: 699; 18: 217; 20: 295, 754. There were economic as well as moral motives for the formation and organization of these clubs.
54 Report of Latour-Lamontagne, in Caron, *Paris pendant la Terreur*, I, 150.

led by Claire Lacombe, demanded in September 1793 that every woman wear a tricolor cockade. Manifesting their opposition to those who were politically motivated, the fishwives and charwomen of Les Halles physically attacked those who appeared with the national colors. The Convention then responded by decreeing that henceforth no woman would "be required to wear the national cockade."[55] Later the Convention reacted with sterner measures as a result of feminine participation in the so-called "hunger insurrection" of Prairal, Year III. It decreed that women be prohibited from attending political gatherings and no longer be allowed to gather in the streets in groups of more than five.[56] Thus, as of May 1795, the rights of women may be said to have swung full circle in the six years since May 1789, from inequality to equality and back to inequality again.

Was the same true of divorce? Despite canonical injunctions against it during the Old Regime, there had come into use an ingenious device which had almost the same effect as divorce. Known as the practice of "Judicial Separation," it was often referred to as "*divertium.*" It was explained by Louis Mercier as follows:

> The word "divertium" ... served to designate [the appointment of an] ecclesiastical judge in certain settled cases: adultery of the wife, serious ill treatment on the part of the husband and finally, apostasy, or heresy of one of the spouses [spiritual fornication]. The adultery of the husband excused that of the wife, and carried with it separation, if the wife, without blame on her part, demanded it. Co-habitation and the conjugal duty ceased to be obligatory, but reconciliation was possible.[57]

By means of "divertium," therefore, unhappily married couples had been able to enjoy the privileges and advantages of divorce—with, apparently, few of its dangers or pitfalls.

This practice may perhaps explain why among the *cahiers* of 1789 only one has been found favoring a divorce law as such—the dubious one presented at the instigation of the Duc d'Orléans, whose motives let alone his actions, were always suspect and difficult to explain.[58]

55 Alexandre Tuetey, *Répertoire général des sources manuscrites de l'histoire de Paris pendant la Révolution française*, 11 vols. (Paris, 1890-1914), 9: nos. 1306, 1314, 1348, 1352, 1355, 1365, September 14, 15, 19, 20, and 21, 1793; Report of Latour-Lamontagne in Caron, *Paris pendant la Terreur*, I, 149, 150.

56 *Moniteur*, 17: 1-2, 717; 18: 285. See also Ernest F. Henderson, *Symbol and Satire in the French Revolution* (New York, 1912), p. 438. Henderson comments, "This ... National convention ... had the courage—for it takes courage to oppose a whole sex and deprive it of rights long enjoyed but not worthily exercised—to decree that women might no longer be present at any political assembly...."

57 Mercier, *Picture*, p. 156. See also Jean B. Brissaud, *A History of French Private Law*, trans. R. Howell (Boston, 1912), p. 145.

58 *Instruction donnée par S. A. S. Mgr le duc d'Orléans* (1789), in Sagnac, *Législation civile*, pp. 282-83, n. 8. See also Hyslop, *Guide*, pp. 59-61. Hyslop points out that although the Third Estate of Marseilles accepted the instructions of the Duke and included a request for divorce, *in actuality, its representatives subsequently opposed divorce.* See also Albert Maurin, *Galérie historique de la révolution ..., 1787 à 1815* (Paris, 1849-1950), I, 93, 293-312. The actions of the Duc d'Orléans have not as yet been satisfactorily explained.

Despite this lack of evidence of any agitation for a divorce decree, there existed a "climate of opinion"[59] favoring it as well as civil marriage. The concept of divorce, moreover, had always been implicit in the doctrine of natural rights of the *philosophes* which, when carried to its logical conclusion, meant that women should have the same rights as men, both in private and in public.[60]

Although evidence for determining the actual feelings of the French concerning divorce before 1789 is not conclusive, there is little doubt that an increasing and incessant demand for that right developed after that date. The subject of divorce continually came up for discussion after 1789 in the legislative debates and in print.[61] Simultaneously, in the National Assembly women began to present resolutions and petitions demanding legislation either to abolish the dowry altogether, or, at the minimum, to prevent a husband's spending it recklessly after he had access to it; to prohibit the confinement of young girls in convents; to clarify the rights of women; and, finally, to give women the right of divorce.[62] Immediately recognizing the growing unrest among the people as well as the consequences of the lack of a marriage and divorce law,[63] the Constituent Assembly on August 5, 1790 set up two new agencies, *le bureau de paix* and *le tribunal de famille*. The former arbitrated between estranged couples in a lawsuit, and the latter prevented the separation of an estranged couple if such a separation were detrimental to the other members of the family—particularly if children were involved.[64]

Whatever the extent of this agitation, it was not until September 20, 1792 that the Legislative Assembly decreed that marriage was a civil contract dissoluble by divorce.[65] Philippe Sagnac gives the *raison d'être* for the establishment of the Divorce law:

> Divorce was the natural consequence of the new concept of marriage as a [civil] contract. . . . As a social theory, divorce was necessary [in order] . . . to insure the happiness of society as well as that of the married individuals [an unhappy union should not be forced to continue]; . . . to deliver women from marital despotism; [and] . . . to guarantee liberty of conscience and of worship by leaving each person free to use the law at will. . . . Furthermore, if the object of divorce was the happiness of mar-

59 Becker, *Everyman*, pp. 5-28.
60 *Archives parlementaires*, 4: 256; 5: 641.
61 *Moniteur*, 2, 228, 315. See also Godechot, *Les Institutions*, p. 212.
62 *Moniteur*, 2, 262-63, 315-16.
63 Duvergier, *Collection*, I, 33-35. The Constituent Assembly between August 4 and 11, 1789 had suspended *all* the laws of the Old Regime. Marriage and divorce, therefore, were only two of the many legal gaps that the Assembly was rushing to fill.
64 *Archives parlementaires*, 17: 616. "La Bureau de paix: elle tend à calmer les passions de deux qui s'engagent trop inconsidérement dans les procès." *Le tribunal de famille* was "required to resolve, without notoriety, those disagreements between married couples . . . who, without such redress, often so scandalized society [as to lead] to the ruin of an entire family." It was also given jurisdiction in the matter of young people who had gone astray.
65 Duvergier, *Collection*, IV, 476-82.

ried people, of families, and of the state, then such a law was not contrary to the precepts of religion.[66]

Thus, as of September 1792, in the matter of divorce as well as in marriage the basic revolutionary tenets of "equality" and "secularization"[67] were carried to their logical conclusion—at least in law. The dreams and theories so long discussed and anticipated during the Old Regime among the intelligentsia seemed about to become realities. Divorce had become legal. Would it result in a rush to take advantage of this law?

While that was true in the Year II, and although the Year III saw a tremendous upsurge in their number, divorces dropped sharply, in the Year IV and continued downward until they reached their lowest point in the Year XII. In Toulouse, for example, "after the initial peak in the Year II [about 1 divorce to 8 marriages] the rate fell rapidly to a ratio of about 1 divorce to 15 marriages."[68] Even then the great majority of divorces were apparently confined almost exclusively to the larger cities in France. In Paris alone, 5,987 divorces were granted between January 1793 and June 1795.[69] Why the divorce rate dropped so markedly after 1794 is difficult to determine. One reason may have been the influence of sans-culottism with its emphasis on family fidelity. Another may have been the general uncertainty and insecurity of the period, which would have discouraged plunging into new ventures. The need to find human warmth when so many comforting ties were being broken might be another explanation.

Perhaps some light is shed on the drop in the divorce rate by the fact that a small but vociferous minority continued to make evident its general disapproval of divorce throughout the entire Revolution.[70]

66 "Décret 20 septembre 1792 sur le divorce," in Sagnac, *Législation civile*, p. 288.
67 Hyslop, *French Nationalism*, 101-107. This secularism was evident in the *cahiers* themselves in that they reflected a demand for the "elimination of the Christian element in the theory of the state." Furthermore, writes Hyslop, the "widespread concern for *moeurs* and ethics rather than for church doctrine ... [and]... the development of utilitarian ideas in connection with the churches, were all evidence of secularism as early as 1789. . . ."
68 Wesley D. Camp, *Marriage and the Family in France since the Revolution* ... (New York, 1961), pp. 74-75, 124. Camp infers the national rate of divorce in France from the statistics "pertaining to the city of Toulouse, where the statistics were apparently more complete than elsewhere." Roderick G. Phillips, "Le Divorce en France à la fin du XVIIIe siècle," *Annales, économies, sociétés, civilisations*, 34 (February 1979), 385-98, argues that divorce was largely an urban phenomenon. Four or five times as many divorces took place in towns as in the countryside because of the "material" circumstances, i.e., because of the presence of inns, *pensions*, and furnished rooms, none of which was available in rural areas. Moreover, in the countryside a woman had to surrender her employment with her residence. Furthermore, the increase of population in the countryside encouraged the growth of individualism as young people tended to break away from the traditional family unit, now in a state of economic decline.
69 Camp, *Marriage*, p. 124. See also Sagnac, *Législation civile*, p. 293.
70 *Moniteur*, 11: 404. In February 1792, M. Dumolard, one deputy among several, had presented one of the most typical arguments in the Legislative Assembly itself in an

Plays expressing bourgeois and republican sentiment, such as the popular "Alceste à la Campagne," ran continuously, even during the Terror.[71] Numerous engravings,[72] all extolling the benefits of a happy marriage and denouncing divorce as destructive of family life, had wide currency throughout the Revolution. This apparent distaste for divorce and the prevailing sentiment for maintaining a marriage once it was contracted was evinced even by the otherwise radical Chaumette. He kept handy a pretty speech which he invariably delivered to those married couples he thought could be persuaded to repent of a contemplated divorce, thus permitting themselves to be reconciled:

> Young newlyweds, whom a tender engagement has already reunited, [remember] that it is upon the altars of Liberty that the flames of Hymen have been rekindled for you. Marriage is no longer a yoke, nor a chain; it is no more [nor less] than it ought to be: the achievement of the high purposes of nature, the discharge of a pleasant duty... which every citizen owes his country....[73]

Not long after the passage of the decrees on Marriage and Divorce, many abuses of the divorce law came to the attention of the National Convention. One of the most frequent and persistent, noted quite early by Roland, concerned women whose husbands were *émigrés*. He confirmed the generally held suspicion that women used the divorce decree as a means of divesting themselves of a detrimental marriage to an *émigré*, not only because it was an unpopular liaison in 1792 and especially dangerous during the Terror, but also because divorce served as a means of retaining a share in the *émigré*'s property, which otherwise would have been confiscated by the state.[74] While these "divorces of convenience" could be excused as "business arrangements," they were nevertheless condemned, as might be expected, by the revolutionaries as both illegal and immoral. Needless to say, they placed the Church itself in a moral dilemma. How viable were marriages contracted under the Old Regime and now dissolved under the divorce decree? It was not an easy question to answer, especially when churchmen were sympathetic to the precarious position of their flock. Typical are the examples of Beaumarchais,[75] who managed to serve

attempt to prevent hasty marriages and to stop the trend toward divorce. Although the argument did not prevent either, it was not forgotten.

71 Ibid., 9: 50.
72 Jean Robiquet, *La vie quotidienne au temps de la Révolution* (Paris, 1938), p. 86.
73 *Moniteur*, 13: 614; 16: 622. See also Maurin, *Galérie*, I, 295-96, and *Journal de Perlet*, October 1792, in Robiquet, *La vie*, pp. 87-88.
74 *Archives parlementaires*, 53: 139-40.
75 Georges Lamaître, *Beaumarchais* (New York, 1949), pp. 324-30; 336-37. Although Beaumarchais had been sent on an official secret mission to Holland and England in May 1793, his name, nevertheless, appeared on the *émigré* lists. In order to protect their property, her person, and her daughter, even though the Reign of Terror was actually over by then, Mme Beaumarchais in October of 1794 divorced Beaumarchais. They did not remarry until May 1797, by which time their daughter had married and both their property and their persons were safe.

safely both the Monarchy and the Revolution as a secret agent, and of the Countess de Flahaut, long-time mistress of Talleyrand and passionately pursued "companion" of Gouverneur Morris.[76]

As Sagnac makes clear, "Many wives of *émigrés* began to demand divorces in order to regain their share of the communal goods previously requisitioned by the Motherland.... Many others at the same time profited by the absence of their husbands in the army."[77]

What complicated the problem of the *émigrés*, as well as others who desired to be married, divorced, or remarried, was the requirement of the divorce decree itself—residence.[78] During the Revolution, especially at the time of the Terror, many people were forced to change their original place of residence—in fact, as is known, many of the *émigrés* had left France altogether. By the subsequent Law of 27 Germinal, Year II, in order to make certain that *émigrés* would not be able to circumvent the original law, marriages and divorces had to be performed at the place of original residence.[79] But it was not until 11 Vendémaire, Year III, that the National Convention took cognizance of the difficulties presented by this requirement and provided that *émigrés* and others could re-enter France at designated *places frontières et maritimes* in order to declare, or legalize, either a marriage or a divorce. The "catch" was, however, that they had first to present a "certificate from the place [*municipalité*] where they have been living since the passage of this law [Law of 27 Germinal] to the effect that they have caused no disturbance."[80]

Of course, there were also divorces based on other than legal and political grounds. One interesting example is found in a letter to the National Convention from the municipality of Pont-Croix which cites the admirable precedent set by a certain Citizen Allain who had di-

76 "Letter to Jefferson," January 6, 1793, in Gouverneur Morris, *The Diary and Letters of Gouverneur Morris, Minister of the United States to France*, ed. and trans. A. C. Morris (Boston, 1939), II, 600. Morris recorded how, after he had earlier helped the Countess to escape to England, she then desired to return to France. She had contemplated divorcing her "soon to be guillotined" husband in order to make her return to France safe and possible. Her hopes were not to be fulfilled. In the same letter Morris pointed out that, "As the king was condemned [formally on January 20 and immediately executed on the following day], prudence triumphed over nostalgia and the divorce idea."

77 Sagnac, *Législation civile*, p. 293.

78 Duvergier, *Collection*, IV, 93-95. The decree of April 8, 1792 had specified "*émigration*" as one of the seven grounds for divorce as well as for the confiscation of *émigré* property by the state.

79 *Moniteur*, 14: 158, 599; 20: 256. In September and November of 1792 the question of whether to forestall the divorced wives of *émigrés* from receiving the property of their former husbands came up for heated discussions in the National Convention. See Camp, *Marriage*, pp. 71-72, who also indicates the addition of "aristocracy and uncivic conduct" as among the unusual grounds for divorce, along with "emigration."

80 *Moniteur*, 22: 112. This decree also provided that "such a person shall be expected to justify to the Committees of Surveillance that the object of his re-entry is solely to declare either his marriage or his divorce...."

vorced "a wife of sixty years of age, and had formed a new relationship with a young female companion, in order to increase the number of defenders of liberty." In obvious admiration of this act, the city fathers of Pont-Croix, on 11 Floréal, Year II, proceeded to request from the Convention a new decree to the effect that "Those women whose age and [physical] condition might prevent their having more children should be permitted, for the love of their country, to separate from those husbands [who were still] capable of exercising their function [in this respect]."[81] Furthermore, and more seriously, divorce was also recommended as a means of freeing "victims of cupidity, ambition, and caprice from the tyranny of their parents."[82] A final argument in favor of divorce was summed up in a letter to the editor of the *Moniteur*: "An unhappy marriage is a bad example for children. . . . Divorce will do away with scandals, adultery, and unhappiness."[83]

By July 1795, however, the attitude toward divorce had become generally unfavorable, reflecting the general conservatism of the Year III. One deputy, in fact, demanded that the divorce law be returned to the Committee on Legislation so that it could be made stricter, because as it then stood, "it was more a game of chance than a law."[84] Later students of the French Revolution—Sagnac, Godechot, and Lefebvre—have lent support to the view that a generally unfavorable attitude toward divorce existed. "Revolutionary legislation . . . only . . . increased the flood of corruption which invaded the cities and especially Paris,"[85] wrote Sagnac. For Godechot the attack on the divorce law came because it was in "flagrant violation of . . . the principle of equality contained in the Declaration of Rights of 1789,"[86] since men were granted divorces more easily than women. Lefebvre interpreted the reaction as resulting from the bourgeoisie's return to political power in 1794:

> The Thermidoreans did not have the time to give the bourgeoisie . . . the social character which it would later receive in the form of the Civil Code. . . . It is clear that morals, and above all the concept of what morals ought to be, had not developed at all as one would have imagined under the liberal principles proclaimed in 1789, especially as far as women were concerned.[87]

81 J. Guillaume (ed.), *Procès-verbaux du Comité d'Instruction publique de la Convention Nationale* (Paris, 1891-1907), IV, 296.
82 *Moniteur*, 2: 228.
83 Ibid., 7: 112. This letter was written by a woman who was admittedly unhappy in her marriage.
84 Ibid., 25: 291.
85 Sagnac, *Législation civile*, p. 293.
86 Godechot, *Les Institutions*, p. 599.
87 Georges Lefebvre, *The Thermidoreans*, trans. Robert Baldick (New York, 1964), pp. 217-18. Lefebvre continues: "The Jacobins often had been puritans, [but] rarely feminists." For two of the opposite and extremist views, cf. W. A. Schmidt (ed.), *Tableaux de la revolution française sur les papiers . . .* , 3 vols. (Leipzig, 1867-70), II, 81; and Edmé Champion et al., *La Révolution française, 1789-1799* (Paris, 1896), 8: 488.

It is clear, therefore, that the revolutionists wanted to transform society from an ecclesiastical to a secular one—at least in respect to the institutions of marriage and divorce. This, in turn, implied a sincere willingness to accept women on an equal basis with men during the early part of the Revolution, and especially during the Terror. Similarly, evidence seems to confirm the existence of constant conflicts between ideals and practices as revealed in legislation proposed, debated, and passed concerning marriage, divorce, and women's rights even when intentions were at their best.

Although marriage as an institution was secularized, it withstood most of the vicissitudes and transformations engendered by the French Revolution, especially during the Terror. Recast as a civil contract, its role as a sacrament of the church was hardly affected, however. Similarly, although divorce was also secularized and legalized, no appreciable increase in its incidence is evident, except during the Terror. In fact, immediately after the Terror, there was a remarkable *decrease* observed. Thus, except during the Terror and despite the successful transition from ecclesiastical to secular control of marriage and divorce, no overall radical change in the habits of the French in these areas can be discerned.[88]

Schmidt represents the secularization of divorce as one of the means of bringing about the greater corruption of morals: "divorce was elevated—along with adultery—to the dignity of a former religious sacrament." Champion criticizes the divorce decree as contributing to "the disorganization of the family, [because] divorce became, in a few years, the dissolving ingredient of civil marriage."

88 Lefebvre, *Thermidoreans*, p. 218: "The French people, on the whole, went on living as they always had lived."

Section Roi-de-Sicile and the Fall of the Monarchy

MORRIS SLAVIN

Among the classic works of the French Revolution are the studies of Fritz Braesch, who examined the political life of the Parisian sections shortly before the fall of the monarchy and immediately thereafter. In his monumental study of the Paris Commune he analyzed the factional oscillations of the general assemblies and their leaders of both Right and Left. Characterizing some sections as conservative and others as democratic, he concluded that Roi-de-Sicile was "moderately conservative." His judgment was based on the position taken by its general assembly relative to the resolution of section Mauconseil no longer to recognize Louis XVI as King of the French. That Braesch was uncertain of his own presentation may be determined from his admission that "during the night of 9 to 10 [August], one finds, not without astonishment" the section's representatives sitting in the Hôtel de Ville.[1] This "astonishment" on the author's part raises the question to what degree of accuracy his analysis of the political complexion of the section remains valid. Braesch's work remains valuable, of course, whether a section is characterized "moderately conservative" or "moderately democratic." How much difference, after all, is there between these two terms in time of revolution? Without engaging in a meaningless semantic argument, therefore, it might still be worthwhile to apply other standards (in addition to the section's position on the Mauconseil resolution), which might gauge more accurately the political shifts in Roi-de-Sicile. It is the purpose of this essay, therefore, to examine the political fluctuations and the revolutionary leaders responsible for them, in order, if possible, to arrive at a more accurate judgment of the section's political tendencies. A closer examination of the struggle within section Roi-de-Sicile, moreover, ought to reflect, in general, the course of this contest in other sections of the capital.

    Section Roi-de-Sicile, known later as Droits-de-l'Homme, had been formed out of district Petit-Saint-Antoine and a portion of Blancs-

---

1 Fritz Braesch, *La Commune de dix août 1792: Etude sur l'histoire de Paris du 20 juin au décembre 1792* (Paris, 1911), pp. 116, 225.

Manteaux.[2] Located in the center of the capital, not far from the Hôtel de Ville,[3] its thirty-one streets and alleys where 12,000 to 14,000 inhabitants were concentrated,[4] covered an area of approximately 1.1 square miles.[5] In 1790 its active citizens numbered 1,699, slightly more than 2% of all active citizens of Paris.[6] The Marais quarter as a whole, of which the section was a part, reflected wide differences in wealth. While the nobility, which formed but 5% of the population held almost 75% of the real and personal property, the artisans who composed 17% had a mere 1% of the wealth.[7] The flight of the nobility during the early days of the Revolution was bound, therefore, to disorganize the economic life of the section because all classes were linked to it. In 1791 there were at least 1,031 working people employed by sixty-seven master craftsmen or merchants in the section.[8] The poor numbered about 10%.[9]

It was the political and military crisis during the summer of 1792 that radicalized section Roi-de-Sicile. On July 11 the country was pro-

2 For the organization of the districts, see Archives de Paris (hereafter A. de P.), 1AZ 113, *Etats-Généraux convocation des habitans du tiers-état de la ville et faux-bourgs de Paris* (15 avril 1789), 24 pp.; Bibliothèque historique de la Ville de Paris (hereafter B.H.V.P.), 100.65, Districts (en général), a collection of twenty-three brochures. See No. 110 bis, *Supplément de la Feuille*, no. 23, p. 1153 (20 avril 1789), and pp. 1160-61.
3 B.H.V.P., Cen Verniquet, *Atlas du plan gén'l de la Ville de Paris* (1791), map no. 37. See the report of Gossin (22 juin 1790) on the organization of Paris in forty-eight sections in *Archives parlementaires de 1787 à 1860* (hereafter A. P.), première série, ed. M. J. Mavidal and M. E. Laurent (Paris: 1879-continuing), 16: 433; Jean B. Duvergier (ed.), *Collection complète de lois, décrets, ordonnances, règlements, avis du conseil d'état . . . de 1788 à 1830 . . .* , 106 vols., 2d ed. (Paris, 1834-1906), 1: 179-90.
4 Archives Nationales (hereafter A. N.), F⁷3688⁴, "Etat général de la population de Paris nombre des citoyens." Other sources give different figures. A. N., F²⁰ 381 and A. N., F²⁰* 19 of 11 Fructidor, An III (August 28, 1794) give 11,015. A. N., F¹¹ 1181 cites 11,488 for 6 Nivôse, An IV (December 27, 1796).
5 Marcel Reinhard, *Nouvelle histoire de Paris: La Révolution 1789-1799* (Paris, 1971), p. 414. Marché-Saint-Pierre was formerly no. 31, section Roi-de-Sicile numbering 210,000 sq. meters.
6 Etienne Charavay, *Assemblée électorale de Paris 18 novembre 1790-15 juin 1791*, 3 vols. (Paris, 1890), 1: Préface, p. ix.
7 Two recent studies on the Marais nobility and bourgeoisie are B.H.V.P., Per. 8°, 1040, D. Roche, *Recherches sur la noblesse parisienne au milieu du XVIIIe siècle*, "La Noblesse du Marais," in *Actes du quatre-vingt-sixième congrès nationale des sociétés savantes* (Montpellier, 1961; Paris, 1962), pp. 541-78; and Bibliothèque Nationale (hereafter B.N.), Lc¹⁸ 466 bis (1959) 8°; M. Vovelle and D. Roche, "'Bourgeois, rentiers, proprietaires: Elements pour la définition d'une catégorie sociale," in *Actes du quatre-vingt-quatrième congrès national des sociétés savantes* (Dijon, 1959; Paris, 1960), pp. 419-52.
8 Fritz Braesch, "Essai de statistique de la population ouvrière de Paris vers 1791," *La Révolution française* (1912), 63: 289-321, gives the figure of 1,028, p. 315, but is in error by 3. The list of workers utilized by Braesch is A.N., F³⁰ 145, "Administration des finances. Echanges d'assignats contre numéraire pour faciliter le paye des ouvriers." It is incomplete, as it omits 11 bakers, 35 butchers, and 67 cobblers. See A. de P., 4 AZ 53 (October 20, 1793); A.N., D III, 256³, d. 10, pièce 59 (19 Prairial, Year III [June 7, 1795]); and A. de P., 4 AZ 356 (9 Vendémiaire, Year III [September 30, 1794]).
9 B. N., Lc² 786, *Journal de la Montagne*, 144 (17 Germinal, An II [April 6, 1794]), p. 1162.

claimed to be in danger.[10] The distinction between active and passive citizens began to disappear as the sections and the National Guard became more democratic. It was impossible to maintain the old division when all Frenchmen were expected to shed their blood equally for the *patrie*. The agitation for universal manhood suffrage now mounted in intensity. On July 13 the Legislative Assembly revoked the suspension of the mayor of Paris, Jérôme Pétion, for his alleged role in permitting the armed demonstration of June 20, 1792 against the King. The Fédérés issued their famous address demanding the suspension of Louis on July 23[11] and the same day commissioners of thirty-three sections created an organ of insurrection, virtually an illegal Commune.

The sections had been made "permanent" on July 25,[12] i.e., they were given the right to convoke themselves and to meet as often as they deemed necessary, without prior consent of higher authorities. The grenadiers, the elite troops of the National guard, were suppressed on July 30. This egalitarian tendency was strengthened further by the admission into the armed forces and the sectional assemblies of workers and petty bourgeois with their pikes. To coordinate this movement a Central Bureau of Correspondence was established by the municipality stimulating the energies of the sections by its circulars and reports.[13] Shortly thereafter the revolutionaries received help from an unexpected source. The Duke of Brunswick's manifesto, threatening the total destruction of Paris, helped set the stage for the overthrow of the King.

During the decisive days preceding the fall of Louis XVI section Roi-de-Sicile became an arena wherein republicans and monarchists fought one another. This may be seen as early as June 20, 1792, the anniversary of the tennis court oath, when armed demonstrators invaded the Tuileries in a vain effort to force Louis to surrender his veto power. Although a number of officers and privates (the professional soldiers), were critical of the role of the municipal government, the vast majority of the section's armed force had marched in support of their comrades in arms from faubourgs Saint Antoine and Saint Marcel.[14] Yet its general assembly had passed a motion to send delegates to the two radical faubourgs "to invite them to maintain the peace and the

10 A. P., 46: 110-11 (July 4, 1792). The definitive text appeared the following day, pp. 133-34.
11 Ibid., 47: 69-70.
12 Ibid., 47: 143, on a motion of Thuriot. A. N., AD XVI, 70 (July 28, 1792); B.H.V.P., 104.095 (July 28, 1792), a printed sheet headed "Loi relative à la permanence des Assemblées de section [sic] dans Paris."
13 Braesch, *Commune*, pp. 104-34, passim; Ernest Mellié, *Les Sections de Paris pendant la Révolution française (21 mai 1790-19 Vendémiaire an IV): Organisation-Fonctionnement* (Paris, 1898), p. 116.
14 A. N., BB[30] 17, "Pièces relatives à l'événement de 20 juin 1792."

most perfect solidarity without which society could not exist."[15] This
conservative resolution illustrates the divided feelings of the section.
While some were invading the chateau of the King others were ad-
monishing the demonstrators to maintain law and order.

During the last week of July the section had adopted a resolution
that it would act according to circumstances,[16] a non-committal position
reflecting the indecisive struggle between the two factions. On July 31
section Mauconseil adopted its famous motion for the dethronement
of the King,[17] to which section Roi-de-Sicile declared its adherence on
August 2. The following day (August 3), it participated in the delegation of the sections, with mayor Pétion at their head, bearing a petition
to the Legislative Assembly against royalty. The appeal demanded the
dethronement of Louis, in line with the resolution of Mauconseil, and
had been signed by the section's president and future police commissioner, Pierre Auzolles.[18] This trend was completely reversed the next
day, August 4,[19] and on the following day, the section called on the
municipal authorities to maintain order.[20] The directory of the department gratefully acknowledged this conservative position and con-
gratulated Roi-de-Sicile for its resistance to the "deviations of a factious
section."[21]

The course of this struggle is made even clearer in the adoption
and partial repudiation of Jean Varlet's motion to dethrone the King,
introduced by him in the general assembly, on August 5. The petition
embodying it was presented to the Legislative Assembly the next day,
signed, appropriately enough, on the Champs de Mars, by Fédérés and
a great number of ordinary citizens. It began: "The country is in

15 B.H.V.P., MS. 806, fol. 300 (23 juin 1792). I could not find reference to this
    resolution in Braesch.
16 B. N., Lb[40] 3442, Fritz Braesch, *Procès-Verbaux de l'assemblée générale de la section des
    Postes 4 décembre 1790-5 septembre 1792* (Paris, 1911), p. 148, read by section Postes on
    July 29. Braesch is not acquainted, however, with the contents of this resolution.
    There is no mention of it in Louis Mortimer-Ternaux, *Histoire de la Terreur, 1792-
    1794, d'après des documents authentiques et inédits*, 7 vols. (Paris, 1868-1881), 2 (second
    edition, 1870), which deals with the events leading up to the overthrow of the
    monarchy.
17 The resolution stated that Louis had lost the confidence of the nation. The section no
    longer recognized him as King of the French. Cited by Mortimer-Ternaux, *Histoire*,
    2, 174-75. The full version of the resolution is in P. J. B. Buchez and P. C. Roux
    (eds.), *Histoire parlementaire de la Révolution française*, 40 vols. (Paris, 1834-1838), 16,
    246-48.
18 *A. P.*, 47: 425-27 (August 3, 1792).
19 Mortimer-Ternaux, 2: 430. Mortimer-Ternaux lists 14 sections as adhering to the
    resolution, 16 rejecting it, 10 taking no action on it, and 8 leaving no record of their
    vote. Ibid., 2: 443-44. The Assembly rejected the resolution and invited all to abide by
    the law. A.N., AD XVI, 70 (August 4, 1792).
20 Alexandre Tuetey, *Répertoire général des sources manuscrites de l'histoire de Paris pendant
    la Révolution française*, 11 vols. (Paris, 1890-1914), vol. 4, no. 2074 (August 9, 1792).
21 Ibid., Vol. 4, no. 2076 (August 9, 1792). The letter was written by Roederer, the
    procureur-général-syndic of the department to sections Roi-de-Sicile and Jardin-des-
    Plantes. The contents of their resolutions were communicated to the Assembly where
    they were heard "with interest."

danger; these terrible words mean that we are betrayed."[22] The orator then launched into a sharp attack on royalty and on the role of Louis. "Gentlemen," the speaker challenged, "among you sit some favorites of the court." This brought on a violent outburst from the deputies of the Right. The petitioner continued to attack the "monstrous" power of the King to corrupt and to veto legislation. When he denounced the one-sided "contract" between the people and the King the deputies of the Left and their supporters in the galleries burst into applause. Varlet ended his discourse by proposing to veil the Declaration of the Rights of Man as symbolic of the political state of France, to dethrone Louis, to convoke the primary assemblies, and to introduce universal manhood suffrage.[23] His petition, unanimously adopted by the general assembly of the section the previous day, was to be communicated to the other sections by twenty-four commissioners taken from its assembly.[24]

That Varlet himself was not clear as to the probable outcome of the struggle may be gathered from his statement that "The section . . . [was] yielding to judgment which it [the petition] had undergone and desir[ed] to let public opinion decide on this work."[25] On August 7 conservatism was accentuated further in the section by the resignation of Auzolles as president and his replacement by the local justice of the peace, Louis Fayel. The following day Roi-de-Sicile repudiated the August 4 resolution of section Quinze-Vingts threatening to launch an insurrection if the King were not dethroned. The conservative majority argued that the proposal was unconstitutional because according to the municipal code, sections could not concern themselves with anything but municipal matters, and the use of force was reserved to the mayor and municipal officers.[26] In less than a week the section had thus made a complete turnabout from its resolution of August 2. That the conservatives held the initiative at this time may be gathered from the attack made by a citizen of Mauconseil on Varlet's petition, which had

22 *Réimpression de l'ancien Moniteur depuis la réunion des Etats-Généraux, jusqu'au consulat*, 32 vols. (Paris, 1840-1845), vol. 13, no. 220, p. 340 (August 7, 1792).

23 Ibid., p. 341.

24 B.N., Lb[39] 10728, *Voeux formés par les français libres* (Paris, 1792), 8 pp.; British Museum, F65* (2), same title, place, and date of publication. Varlet's version of his program varies slightly from that contained in the *Moniteur*. He makes sixteen demands instead of twelve. Number 7, for example, asks for 250,000 troops instead of 400,000, but it is essentially the same in all other respects. Braesch gives the full title of the brochure and three editions that he found of this work. *La Commune*, p. 165, n. 2.

25 Cited by Braesch, ibid., p. 166, italicizing the last clause.

26 A.N., C 161, 350, pc. 26 (August 8, 1792). "Extrait des registres des délibérations de l'assemblée générale de la section des Droits-de-l'Homme." This was adopted unanimously and was to be communicated to the National Assembly to demonstrate that the section abided by the Constitution. It was signed by Fayel, president, and Ruquet, secretary. Tuetey, *Répertoire* vol. 4, no. 1991 (August 8, 1792). This was done under the pretext that it had no reason to deliberate on the resolution (*qu'il n'y a pas lieu à délibérer*) and inviting section Quinze-Vingts "to confine itself within the precise provisions of the Constitution," not necessarily a harsh condemnation of its action. Mortimer-Ternaux called this action "an energetic protest," in *Histoire*, 2: 431.

originated in a popular society, he charged. Many of the signatures were fraudulent, he accused, and he cited two names to prove it.[27]

If the democrats had their spokesman in Varlet, the conservatives had their champions as well. One, who simply signed himself "A Citizen of Section du Roi-de-Sicile," argued that although the section contained more than 2,000 active citizens only 100 to 130 had bothered to vote on the question of the abdication of the King. Among the latter were passive citizens and even non-residents, he charged. Accusing the opposition of intimidating the monarchists and then forcing through their own petitions he revealed that they employed the extraordinary commission formed by the thirty-three radical sections since July 23, thus bypassing the legal Commune where they were outnumbered.[28]

Throughout the evening of August 9 the struggle within the assembly of the section continued. Fayel, as president, frustrated the demands of insurrectionists by adjourning the session and carrying off the register of the proceedings to his home. The revolutionists then installed their own president, Paulet, a constitutional priest. Only at 3 a.m. did the assembly, which must have been a mere rump, send three commissioners to the Hôtel de Ville. One of them, Paul Henri Pollet (not to be confused with Paulet), resigned his commission at 8 a.m. on August 10.[29] The victory of the radicals was inconclusive, therefore, until the very moment of the insurrection.

Historians of the insurrection have noted the confusion attending the installation of the extraordinary commissioners who replaced the legally elected Commune and who guided the attack on the Tuileries. It is no wonder, then, that lists of participants who made up the illegal Commune differ. Section Roi-de-Sicile, for example, sent three commissioners to the General Council during the night of August 9 or early morning of the following day. Another three were sent on August 10.[30] All were endowed with full powers to do whatever was necessary to save public affairs.

27 *Moniteur*, vol. 13, no. 222, p. 357 (August 9, 1792). Charles Brunot is the citizen mentioned. Tuetey, *Répertoire*, vol. 4, no. 1987 (August 6, 1792), gives the name as Bruneaut.

28 B.H.V.P., MS.104.095, *Observation sur la demande qui a été fait de la déchéance du Roi* ([Paris], August 6, 1792), 4 pp.

29 Mortimer-Ternaux, *Histoire*, 2: 431. The author says that Pollet feared the responsibility but offers no proof for this remark. This resignation did not prevent Pollet from playing a role as a member of the civil committee nor from being elected to the Commune.

30 A. de P., 1 AZ 146, *Tableau-Général des commissaires des 48 sections qui ont composés le conseil-général de dix août mil sept cent quatre-vingt-douze l'an premier de la République française* (Paris, August 10, 1792), 21 pp. This is the list referred to by Buchez and Roux, *Histoire parlementaire*, 16: 410, which formed the basis for Braesch's study, "Liste, par order alphabétique, des individus ayant fait parti du conseil général de la commune, du 9 août, à minuit, au 17 août soir," *La Commune*, pp. 245-64. Mortimer-Ternaux's work differs in some essential respects with the above. The list of 288 names contains more names than the total membership on the General Council because of the confusion immediately following the events of August 10. Ibid., p. 265.

Who were these men? Most seem to have been family men with fixed residences in the section, holding local government posts, enjoying modest incomes as members of the liberal professions or as artisans with small shops of their own. Paul-Henri Pollet, for example, was thirty-two years old, a school teacher, residing on rue Roi-de-Sicile,[31] and a future member of the section's civil committee. He was replaced almost immediately, on August 10, possibly because he was lukewarm to the attack on the Tuileries. His substitute was Jean Chevalier, appointed by the General Council together with three other men to serve at Temple prison where Louis and his family had been confined.[32] In November Chevalier was given police powers with his colleagues to maintain order in the prison.[33]

Etienne-Pierre Leclerc was fifty-seven years old when he sat on the General Council during the night of August 9-10. Residing on rue des Juifs, he was the father of three children, two of whom participated in the attack on the Tuileries. Because he had been serving as police commissioner of the Commune at the time of the September massacres he was later attacked by the Thermidorians as having been somehow responsible. Employed as clerk-registrar in the Hôtel de Ville and as an assistant to the head of the Bureau of Provisions before July 14, 1789, he was sent to the insurrectionary General Council by his section. As the Revolution unfolded he joined the Cordelier and Jacobin Clubs, the *Société fraternelle des deux sexes*, and the *Club central et electoral*— all the more politically conscious societies of the capital. It was as a member of the latter organization that he prepared for the insurrection. Moving from one modest post to another he occupied a seat on the revolutionary tribunal of the third arrondissement, became director of the jury for six months, then sat on the criminal court. He claimed always to have been on good terms with patriots and was an intimate of Marat.[34]

Leclerc was accused of having stolen a watch from a victim of the September massacres, but successfully refuted this "slander" and was confirmed as a judge shortly thereafter. On 13-14 Messidor, Year II (July 1-2, 1794), he was arrested by the Committee of Public Safety and sent to La Force prison, where he remained until the 9th of Thermidor. Although released by the Committee of General Security he was not

31 The *Tableau-Général* gives no information on Pollet.
32 Tuetey, *Répertoire*, vol. 8, no. 720 (September 10, 1792). See also ibid., vol. 6, no. 418 (August 30, 1792).
33 Ibid., vol. 8, no. 781 (November 18-21, 1792). Braesch's reference to Tuetey, *Répertoire*, vol. 6, no. 569 is in error as it deals with a justice of the peace, Le Chevalier, mentioned by the committee of section Roule, presumably its surveillance committee.
34 A.N., F⁷ 4774⁹, d.l, "Réponse aux questions proposée à [. . .] par le Comité de Sûreté Générale pour Etienne-Pierre Leclerc ci-devant administrateur de la Police de la Commune de 10 Aoust et depuis juge du tribunal du 3e arrondt de Paris détenu à la Force"; Tuetey, *Répertoire*, 5, Introduction, pp. x-xiii. See also the scattered references to him in Braesch's *La Commune*.

restored to full rights of citizenship (i.e., was not rearmed), and, consequently, was not returned to his former position in the Office of National Estates. Leclerc stressed his devotion to the Revolution which had begun with the wrongful seizure of his property by a bishop in an unexplained action. In a summary of his revolutionary conduct he revealed that as one of the commissioners appointed to watch over the imprisoned King he had insisted that Louis be moved into less comfortable, but more secure, quarters. Protesting that he had never signed any petition which threatened to compromise liberty he asserted that he had always behaved properly. He was rearrested by the Thermidorians of the section on 6 Prairial, Year III (May 25, 1795) and was accused of being somehow responsible for a letter sent by the police which, allegedly, had encouraged the massacres. A more specific charge was that he had manifested "indecent joy" at seeing victims of "tyranny" go to their execution. He was then sixty years old. Although there are no documents which mention his ultimate fate, it can be assumed that he was freed with other victims of Thermidorian reaction, shortly before the attempted royalist coup of Vendémiaire.

Jean-Baptiste-Pierre Lenfant resided on rue Saint Antoine. He was elected to the Commune on August 10 and was appointed assistant police administrator at the end of the month. As an administrator of clothing (*administrateur de l'habillement*) he was arrested, probably on a charge of peculation, on 12 Nivôse, Year II (January 1, 1794), by order of the Committee of General Security. Found innocent, he was released on 21 Ventôse (March 11).[35] Like Leclerc, he was rearrested on 6 Prairial, Year III (May 25, 1795), by the Thermidorian assembly of the section for having signed "an infamous letter" as a member of a police administration that had defended the September massacres. Lenfant wrote an eloquent denial of this charge protesting that he had never denounced any "unfortunates," although being aware that many reputations had been made in the section by "vociferous declamations against them."[36] During the unfortunate events of September he had never left the Hôtel de Ville, nor had he ever been a judge in any prison while these horrors were taking place.[37]

35 Archives Préfecture de Police (hereafter A.P.P.) A A/136, fol. 49. Auzolles lifted the seals from his papers on 10 Germinal (March 30).
36 A.N., F⁷ 4774¹⁷, d.l (8 Prairial, Year III [May 28, 1795]). The *procès-verbal* was signed by Grandjean, president of the assembly, and Boudard, secretary. It was revealed that although the letter in question had not been found at Robespierre's home, none of its signatories denied its existence when it had been disclosed to the Convention. This type of reasoning foreshadowed totalitarian frameups in our own day. On the obverse side of this document was a notation that Leclerc recognized the existence of the letter in question, and had only denied signing it, not its existence. Lenfant's denial bears no date, although Tuetey, *Répertoire*, 5, Introduction, p. xiii, places it as sometime in Thermidor.
37 Bibliothèque Victor Cousin (hereafter B.V.C.), MS. 120, fols. 163-65 (7 Prairial 1795 [May 27]).

The civil committee confessed that it knew no witness who could testify that Lenfant had indeed signed the notorious letter, and admitted that no such signatures existed. After the surveillance committee of the seventh arrondissement recommended that Lenfant be freed, the Committee of General Security ordered his provisional release under the surveillance of the section's authorities. Lenfant appealed for full freedom and had his petition endorsed by two Representatives of the People, Roy and Reynaud. There is no indication of the final outcome of his appeal, although it can be assumed that the Committee of General Security hardly would have ignored a petition signed by deputies of the Convention at a time when it was releasing prisoners with far fewer endorsements.[38]

Claude Coulombeau was forty years old, a lawyer by profession, residing on rue des Francs-Bourgeois. He was elected a commissioner on August 10 and shortly thereafter became secretary-registrar of the Commune in which position he served for more than a year. Arrested as a Dantonist in Floréal, Year II (April-May, 1794), he was released after the death of Robespierre. Coulombeau was a prodigious worker as a glance at the thousands of documents transcribed by him reveals. When the General Council complained about certain irregularities he wrote that his work was "immense, beyond human power . . . I am usually at work fourteen hours in the Hôtel de Ville; very often I spend 18 to 20 hours there."[39]

Mareux, *père* resided on rue Saint Antoine. Nothing is known of him except that he was appointed to the assembly of commissioners during the night of August 9-10.[40] The last name carried on the list of the *Tableau-Général* is that of Rumel. He was already sitting in the Hôtel de Ville during the night of August 9-10 (possibly as an observer), when he was elected by the section on August 10. Nothing more is known about him,[41] nor about a commissioner by name of Berle who was also elected the same day.[42]

According to the General Council, of the commissioners listed, all but Pollet and Rumel had fulfilled their duties by remaining at their

38 A.N., F⁷ 4774¹⁷. He was released on 20 Thermidor, Year III (August 7, 1795).
39 Mortimer-Ternaux, *Histoire*, 2: 451 and n. 3. The quotation is from Braesch, *Commune*, p. 277. Braesch calls him an "honnête homme."
40 His name appears in the *Tableau-Général*. Braesch added the "*père*" and considered the possibility that his name might have been Mareuil, *Commune*, p. 258.
41 Mortimer-Ternaux, *Histoire*, 2: 451. Braesch gives the name of Romel as an alternative to Rumel, *Commune*, p. 262.
42 His name is not mentioned in the *Tableau-Général* nor by Mortimer-Ternaux. B.N., MSS, Nouv. acq. fr. 2691, fols. 143-44, mentions him, however. Braesch cites this source in his *La Commune*, p. 246. Mortimer-Ternaux lists only Lenfant, Coulombeau, and Rumel as commissioners, but quotes Buchez and Roux as including Pollet, Leclerc and Mareux. Braesch accepts the list of Buchez and Roux as constituting the "illegal Commune" rather than that of Mortimer-Ternaux. According to Buchez and Roux, 28 sections sent representatives to the Hôtel de Ville, totaling 89 commissioners. Huguenin of section Quinze-Vingts presided over the assembly to which section Roi-de-Sicile sent a representative. Braesch, *Commune*, pp. 222-24.

posts.[43] After August 17, additional commissioners were elected to the Commune, some serving with a clear mandate and others remaining only briefly. In addition to Chevalier, mentioned above, an F. Giraud served as president of the General Council after September 6. He might have been François Giraud who became a member of the Commune on December 2. An order for the arrest of an apprentice banker was signed by him on September 6.[44]

Philippe Hardy was thirty years old, a shoemaker by trade and captain in the armed forces, residing on rue des Juifs. He was arrested on September 21, 1793 for ostensibly giving asylum to a member of the former nobility and for helping a Princess Talmont make her escape from Paris. At the time of his arrest he was employed as a registrar in the police court. On October 2 the revolutionary committee reported that after an examination of his papers it found nothing suspicious. Hardy petitioned for his release from la Force prison citing deputy Réal who could testify to his poverty. On 14 Brumaire, Year II (November 4, 1793), the assistant public prosecutor wrote a letter in his favor, countersigned by the judge of the court of the 17th and 1st arrondissements.[45] It can be assumed that he was freed shortly thereafter.

These commissioners from Roi-de-Sicile sat with others from the "ultra-democratic" sections (to use the characterization of Fritz Braesch), representing those sections which marched against the Tuileries. Collectively they constituted the core of the revolutionary movement against the monarchy. Of the twenty-three sections "moderately democratic" only eight failed to send representatives. On the basis of this analysis it seems difficult to argue that a section which had not sent commissioners to the Hôtel de Ville at the decisive moment of August 9-10 was "moderately democratic" while one which did, like Roi-de-Sicile, was "moderately conservative." Is it not possible to hold that what determined the political complexion of a section was not so much its position on the resolutions of sections Mauconseil and Quinze-Vingts, but rather, its ultimate action during the night of August 9-10? Most conservative sections remained silent and awaited the outcome.[46]

In an apology written shortly after the insurrection, section Roi-de-Sicile replied to accusations made against it by section Quinze-Vingts for its equivocal conduct in the past. Appealing to its critics as old friends who had shed blood in common against "tyranny" it admitted

43 This is indicated by an asterisk placed before each name in the *Tableau-Général*.
44 Tuetey, *Répertoire*, vol. 7, no. 1234 (September 16, 1792). Braesch is careful to explain that his "Liste des membres de la commune révolutionnaire nommés après le 17 août 1792" is quite tentative and uncertain. *La Commune*, pp. 641-43.
45 A.N., F⁷ 4739, d.1; A.P.P., A B/327, p. 420 (September 22, 1793). It is difficult to say if this Hardy was the same man who was elected to the civil committee.
46 Braesch, *La Commune*, pp. 224-25.

that there had been two sections formerly—that of "the patriots" and that of "counter-revolutionaries." Now, however, there was but one section of patriots whose deliberations were open to the public. The authors hastened to repudiate all past resolutions contrary to the principles of liberty as the work of the former "cabal" in the section.[47]

The intention of the announcement was to dispel the charge of uncivic behavior made against the section and to reassure its friends in the neighboring sections that the conservative party had, indeed, been defeated. Indirectly, it must have acted as a warning to the former members of the "cabal" that the democrats were firmly in control as manifested by the unanimous support of the active sectionnaires who adopted the address. Moderation, at least as defined in pre-August 10 terms, was now out of favour; conservatism, needless to say, was even more so.

The revolutionary waves, however, were to display troughs as well as crests. One could never be certain, after all, of a decisive victory. The militants surely must have known that in times of flux, nothing was permanent. When Pétion resigned as mayor, after being elected to the Convention, section Droits-de-l'Homme (as Roi-de-Sicile was called after August 21, 1792), together with Quatre-Nations, Faubourg-Montmartre, Luxembourg, and Arsenal asked him to remain in his former position. Had the moderates in these sections raised their heads again? They seem to have found their voice in him, for Pétion was not the leader of the more militant revolutionaries.[48] After the September massacres there was a predictable reaction in some sections, and a number of them sent their commissioners to the General Council on the evening of September 9 to discuss the matter. Among these were delegates of section Droits-de-l'Homme.[49] The vacillation of the section was to continue, despite "unanimous" resolutions to the contrary. Democrats and conservatives were ultimately dependent on the general course of the Revolution, as its history was to prove.

The commissioners of the sections, the "illegal Commune," sat in an adjoining room of the Hôtel de Ville where the legal Commune was holding its sessions. At first they waited for a majority of delegates to arrive. After some preliminaries, however, the legal Commune approved the action of the sections which had replaced their representatives to the General Council. Then the newly elected representatives passed a resolution stating that:

47 B.N., Lb⁴⁰ 3246, *Adresse des citoyens de la section du Roi-de-Sicile à leurs frères de la section des Quinze-Vingts et de toutes les sections de Paris* (Paris, n.d.), 1 p. It was signed by Pollet, president, Huguet, secretary, and 300 citizens of the section. This must have been published between August 10 and August 21, 1792 when the section changed its name.

48 Braesch, *Commune*, p. 539: "The moderates wanted to utilize this name [Pétion's], still popular to bring about a change in feeling in their favor."

49 *Feuille de Paris* (September 10, 1792), cited by Braesch, *Commune*, p. 638. The other sections were Tuileries and Invalides.

The assembly of commissioners of the majority of the united sections with full powers to save public affairs . . . decrees that all power formerly held by the Commune should be transferred to itself; that it suspends provisionally, the powers of the General Council of the Commune, and maintains the mayor, the *procureur*, and the sixteen administrators in their functions.[50]

The commissioners had directed their sections to take political and administrative steps to consolidate the success of the insurrection. They ordered the closing of shops, authorized the call to arms, and launched the arrest of suspects.[51] Two commissioners of section Roi-de-Sicile, Claude-Charles Pointard, who was to be elected justice of the peace in Fayel's place, and Philippe Hardy, were authorized by the General Council to requisition the delivery of mattresses from La Force prison to bed-down "citizen-soldiers" from another commune.[52] Although the section's military detachment, the battalion of Petit-Saint-Antoine, had appointed six commissioners to demand weapons and cartridges from its two former commanders[53] (now suspended), there is no indication whether the commissioners were successful. Two of the battalion's commissioners signed the proclamation of the Legislative Assembly to take measures of public safety.[54]

The general assembly of the battalion of Petit-Saint-Antoine elected commissioners to recover the weapons and cartridges in the hands of Jean-Baptiste Herbault and Pierre Mussey, ex-commanders of the Battalion.[55] The following day section Roi-de-Sicile convoked its citizens to hear Herbault justify his actions and to elect a new commander if need be.[56] On August 13 the provisional commander, Norman, invited the battalion to hear the reading of an address to the Legislative Assembly, and requested the section to convoke its general assembly for the purpose of electing a military committee of twelve members,[57] designed to act as a disciplinary body over its armed forces. On September 22 the General Assembly censured its former commanding

50 A.N., C 156, 304, p. 27 (August 10, 1792).
51 A. de P., 4 AZ 959, "commissaires de la Majorité des Sections Réunis avec pleins pouvoirs pour sauver la chose publique" (August 11, 1792). The call was signed by Huguenin as president and Coulombeau, secretary; B.N., MSS, Nouv. acq. fr. 2691, fol. 131, n.d.
52 Fifty-eight mattresses were to be delivered by the concierge of La Force for the soldiers of Montalban. Buchez and Roux, *Histoire parlementaire*, 18: 278.
53 B.N., MSS, Nouv. acq. fr. 2691, fol. 145 (August 10, 1792).
54 B.N., MSS, Nouv. acq. fr. 2691, fol. 143 (August 10, 1792). The proclamation began with "The National Assembly considering that the dangers to the country have reached their high point" then spelled out in 11 articles steps to be taken. The first was that "all houses shall be illuminated." This was signed by "The Commissioners of the section of Roi-de-Sicile at the general assembly of the 48 sections." The signatures are of Leclerc and Berle.
55 Tuetey, *Répertoire*, vol. 4, no. 2176 (August 10, 1792).
56 Ibid., vol. 4, no. 2177 (August 11, 1792) B.N., MSS, Nouv. acq. fr. 2691, fol. 146 (August 11, 1792), signed by Pointard, Collet, and Hugue.
57 Tuetey, *Répertoire*, vol. 4, no. 2268.

officers,[58] although the exact role of the battalion during the morning of August 10 remained unclear.

A coachman declared that he had heard the cannoneers cry "Vive le Roi!" as they attended the review of Swiss troops by the King.[59] This was corroborated by a volunteer serving in the battalion, who added that his comrades and he had difficulty in leaving the chateau.[60] This report was contradicted, however, by another witness who claimed that the cries were "Vive la Nation!"[61] What probably happened was that while the officers of the armed force remained loyal to the monarchy the men were hostile and manifested their opposition as best they could. Lieutenant Amable-Antoine Picard declared to the committee of surveillance that Roederer, the *procureur-général-syndic* of the department warned the troops at 7 a.m., against riotous assemblies, but that a municipal official told them to repel force with force. An hour later the fight with the Swiss troops broke out.[62]

A number of pillagers were arrested and brought before justices of the peace and police commissioners. Some had silver objects which had been stolen from the palace.[63] On August 11 the authorities of the department of Paris, various committees of the sections, secretaries, and police commissioners were all suspended, and justices of the peace were summoned to the bar to justify their conduct. The sections then proceeded to elect new members to replace the suspended officials.[64] This reorganization of the sections, Commune, and department was paralleled by, and intensified by the change in the method of voting. More and more resort was had to the open voice vote, a sure means of intimidating the moderate and royalist opposition. Section Droits-de-l'Homme decided to elect the mayor and the *procureur* in this manner.[65] Other sections shared this way of voting, and demands were raised that all administrative bodies hold their sessions in public so that the people might know those who had their welfare at heart.[66]

58 B.V.C., MS. 120, fol. 132.
59 Tuetey, *Répertoire*, vol. 5, no. 3988 (August 1792).
60 Ibid., vol. 4, no. 2307 (August 11, 1792). Lebeque reported to section Arcis that when the review passed before the King cries of "Vive le Roi" were heard.
61 Ibid., vol. 4, no. 2309 (August 11, 1792). Report of Phulpin of rue de la Verrerie. He claimed that they had to threaten an officer to get out of the Tuileries.
62 Ibid., vol. 4, no. 2328 (August 15, 1792).
63 BB[30] 18, "Journée du 10 août/15 août 1792." The General Council decreed that of the 1,600 l. recovered by citizen Soubiran of section Droits-de-l'Homme, a sum of 100 l, be given him. A.N., F[7] 4408, d. 2 (October 29, 1792).
64 Maurice Tourneux (ed.), *Procès-Verbaux de la commune de Paris (10 août 1792-1er juin 1793)* (Paris, 1894), p. 11.
65 Braesch, *La Commune*, p. 618. Section Arsenal reported that delegates from Droits-de-l'Homme had informed them that the election of the mayor and *procureur* had taken place by roll call. The assembly of Arsenal applauded and adopted a similar resolution. F[7]* 2501, fol. 142 v° cited by Braesch, ibid., p. 618, n. 3.
66 B.N., MSS, Nouv. acq. fr. 2691, fol. 139. Seven commissioners of the Commune reported that after meeting with representatives of the Legislative Assembly the open voice vote "had been happily employed since the regeneration of August 10." In

The General Council also moved in the direction of closer control of delegates from the sections. By insisting that the latter give a report on their expenditures and receipts since August 10 the Council began to supervise their activities more closely. Section Droits-de-l'Homme first heard this demand transmitted to its general assembly on October 22. On November 2 the Commune demanded a list of names and the residences of all commissioners appointed since August 10.[67]

Section Roi-de-Sicile was bombarded by decrees and ordinances of the new authorities. Citizens were ordered to remain under arms, but on August 11 they were free to reopen their shops. The following day it was decreed by the Commune that ecclesiastical garments be prohibited in public. On August 13 the general assembly was convoked to elect twelve commissioners who could assume newly granted powers under the municipal code. The provisional commander of the battalion asked the militia to hear an address to the National Assembly, and to elect a delegation to present it. That same day it was ruled that citizens were free to leave the city if they wished.[68] A few weeks later, however, the section was authorized by the General Council to take all necessary measures to prevent suspects from escaping across the Seine.[69] On the whole, however, the tensions engendered by the insurrection were beginning to ease.

Jean-François Varlet, as one of the leaders of the republican party, advocated prompt measures to dethrone the King, without waiting for the formal convocation of the primary assemblies. In addition, he suggested the removal of the Dauphin from the care of those whose influence might corrupt him. Blood ties, he pointed out, were more important to him at present than the future of a great empire. Only a different type of education could change his present loyalties, something which could be accomplished by a tutor who would teach him that the duty of kings was to defend the weak. Varlet added in his petition to the Legislative Assembly a demand that it enact laws against profiteering and speculation in currency. "Universal peace to all people; harsh war against all tyrants," he concluded.[70]

While petitions and resolutions were being presented to the municipality and the National Legislature, the assembly of the section appointed a commission to repossess its register from the former

---

A.N., D 3, 251-52, d. 5, pcs. 47, 48 (February 28, 1792) there is a petition of 222 names urging the Legislature to make administrative bodies public.

67 B.V.C., MS. 120, fol. 133. When the commissioners met on December 13 only two were absent from the total representing the 48 sections.

68 B.N., MSS, Nouv. acq. fr. 2691, fols. 147, 151. Many of the notices and decrees in this collection are addressed to section Roi-de-Sicile , but these circulars are of a general nature and are meant for all sections.

69 [Noël] Charavay (ed.), *Catalogue d'une importante collection de documents autographes et historiques sur la Révolution française depuis le 13 juillet 1789 jusqu'au 18 Brumaire An VIII* (Paris, 1862), 5e Arrêté de la Commune (September 2, 1792), 1 p. in folio.

70 A.N., C 161, 351 (August 12, 1792); Tuetey, *Répertoire*, vol. 5, no. 17. Numerous citizens endorsed this petition by their signatures.

president, Fayel.[71] On August 21 the section requested to change its name from Roi-de-Sicile to Droits-de-l'Homme, the name it was to retain until 1796. This was accorded by the General Council.[72] The Rights of Man, obviously, held meaning that the obscure King of Sicily no longer possessed. On September 2 Varlet was elected with two other members by the General Assembly to make judicial investigations (*pour faire des perquisitions*) and to receive testimony and declarations by anyone who wished to lodge complaints or give reports of recent events. These would be directed, of course, against moderates and other opponents of the revolutionists in the section.[73]

Throughout the month of September the section adopted measures to regulate its internal life. Its citizens did everything—from patrolling the barriers to finding lodging for the Fédérés, from demanding uniforms for volunteers to the making of haversacks by its women. On September 2 the section was authorized by the General Council to seize horses from persons who had not been licensed by the municipality after August 10. Its new military officers, confirmed in their election by the general assembly, on September 22, reviewed troops departing for the front. The following day, the section's civil committee distributed new civic cards, destined to play an important role in the life of private citizens. On September 27 it unanimously hailed the proclamation of the French Republic and on the 30th drafted an address to the newly elected Convention.[74]

The address reflected suspicion of the preceding two legislative bodies, and, at the same time, patriotic support for the newly constituted Convention. Pointing to past "betrayals" of the people by former legislators who cloaked their evil machinations under the mask of patriotism, the petitioners boldly announced that all this was changed when "the whole people" rose up, guided by the slogan "the annihilation of kings: live free or die." Although the events of August 10 were bloody they had their good effect. The question now was whether the Convention was worthy of its sublime mission. Within the Convention itself were speculators and the factious whose very existence threatened the whole of France. The decree of the Convention which had abolished the monarchy, however, had saved France. Millions of men stood ready to support the Republic, ready to spill their blood for

71 B.N., MSS, Nouv. acq. fr., 2691, fol. 137.
72 Tourneux, *Procès-Verbaux*, p. 49, "this request was received by lively applause."
73 B.H.V.P., MS. 748, fol. 119.
74 B.V.C., MS. 120, fols. 132 and 133. The first entry is for September 10, 1792. On the requisition of horses see A. de P., 4 AZ 966 (September 2, 1792). That there must have been confusion and overlapping in the sometimes frantic efforts to establish a functioning administration after the insurrection may be taken for granted. A letter from the *procureur-général-syndic* to section Droits-de-l'Homme and to others, for example, rejected their complaints that they were not receiving copies of laws and decrees adopted by the Commune. The failure, he wrote, was due to their own negligence, as the municipality was distributing sufficient numbers of copies. B.N., MSS, Nouv. acq. fr. 2691, fol. 221 (September 13, 1792).

the safety of the country. The Convention could rely on them as they swore "to live free or to die."[75] Thus ended this declaration which began critically and concluded on a note of warm support for the new legislature. Yet it must have occurred to more than one deputy sitting in the chamber to wonder who enjoyed the real power, the National Convention or the sections and their Commune?

The political tendency of section Roi-de-Sicile on the eve of August 10, 1792 was uncertain. Two factions, the constitutional monarchists and the republicans, balanced each other. The "unanimous" resolutions adopted by the general assembly prove little, as each side was able to intimidate, expel, or outmaneuver the other. It is possible that in number of adherents they were nearly equal. In revolutionary situations, however, statistics alone cannot determine the outcome of the struggle. Living action, commitment, and determination of the parties involved, organization and leadership—these are more important. The most decisive factor proves to be the general political climate, itself a product of social and economic forces within the country, and the fortunes of war without.

The action of the general assembly of section Droits-de-l'Homme to send official delegates to the Hôtel de Ville a few hours before the attack on the King's chateau was an act of commitment from which revolutionaries could not retreat. Had the action proved abortive, or had it failed, the republicans in the assembly would have suffered the consequences of a monarchical repression. Whatever the nature of their support, both in numbers and in zeal, their action during the early hours of August 10 proved decisive. Moderate conservatives would not have acted in this manner. The political tone in the sectional assembly, however uncertain it might have been before the fall of the monarchy, was transformed overnight. For the next three years it was the committed republicans who were to lead the section.

75 A.N., C 233, 190 (September 30, 1792). A slightly different version is in B.N., LB[40] 1796, and in Lb[40] 1796A, *Addresse présentée à la convention nationale le 30 septembre 1792, l'an 1er de la République française, par les citoyens Gattrez, Oudart, Pointard, Gasnier* (Paris, 1792), 4 pp. This is reproduced in *A.P.*, 52, 243.

The Intellectual Origins of Babouvism

JAMES R. HARKINS

A perpetual problem to the student of revolutions is the relationship between the intellectual milieu or climate of opinion and the outbreak of violence. The problem continues as the revolution progresses; the historian is faced with trying to determine to what degree the revolutionary action is influenced or determined by that same pre-revolutionary consciousness and purposeful articulation of grievances and designs. It is ludicrous to pretend that a conspiracy of ideas and propagandists can push any society into a profound revolt. It is almost as indefensible to ignore ideas altogether and concentrate upon objective factors. Georges Lefebvre cautioned the historian against trying to separate the ideological preparation for the Revolution from the social and economic conditions of the Old Regime. He encouraged our awareness that the link between historical fact and historical action is the human intellect or consciousness. The revolutionary spirit which provided for purposeful historical action cannot be divorced from its intellectual roots; it is this consciousness which maintains the human equation in the revolutionary process.[1]

For the student of history who is most comfortable with objective evidence and conclusive argument, this territory of ideas and motivation is often uneasily skirted. Even when one attacks the problem directly, the results are not altogether satisfying. In searching for the influence of Jean-Jacques Rousseau, Henri Peyre warns us that what we find is more the "following" of Rousseau than genuine disciples.[2] Even when an apparent disciple is firmly seized and held up to the light, it is quite difficult to measure what part of the leaven at work, in fact, stems from Rousseau's political and social ideas.

Gracchus Babeuf, the subject of this essay, is unquestionably a man much influenced by Rousseau, the Rousseau of *Emile*, of *The Discourse on Inequality*, of the *Social Contract*, of *sans-culottes* propaganda

---

1 Lefebvre cites Jaurès as his own source for this insight which runs as a major thread through his own humanitarian framework in approaching the Revolution, although he recognizes that it was not a perception original to Jaurès. Georges Lefebvre, *Etudes sur la Révolution française*, p. 339. See as well *The Coming of the French Revolution*, trans. R. R. Palmer (New York, 1958), p. 43.
2 Henri Peyre, "The Influence of Eighteenth-Century Ideas on the French Revolution," *Journal of the History of Ideas*, 10 (1949), 84.

and pamphleteering. But Rousseau does not create Babeuf. As the essay will consider, a wide variety of experience and ideas goes into the socialist revolutionary of 1796. Still Rousseau is there, and he is there more because of Babeuf's reading than Rousseau's writing. To find Rousseau in Babeuf is not to interpret Rousseau in his own terms but in Babeuf's. It is very much as Kingsley Martin reminded us several years ago when he cautioned that the search for a writer's influence is better carried out in what people think he said than in his original intent and expression.[3] The task, then, is not to prove the validity of Babeuf's interpretation of Rousseau, but to determine if what Rousseau wrote made a difference to Babeuf's career and to his ultimate sociological analysis and conclusions for society. As Babeuf is the subject of the essay, however, the task is to find who else made a major contribution to this analysis and these conclusions. The purpose is to find the intellectual origins of Babeuf's socialism of 1796 and to relate it to the revolutionary political intentions of Babeuf's conspiracy of that year.

In any one revolutionary there is bound to be a variety of profound experiences at work before and after the outbreak of revolution. This experience is both verbal and non-verbal, i.e., it is the result of logical and systematic disputation in the spoken or printed word and it is the gradual layering of social discontent, social anger, social frustration. These experiences are in constant interaction so that the revolutionary consciousness-raising taking place is not a singular experience but a complex one. It is true that the interrelated experiences can vary a great deal. The cerebral experience of Trotsky is of primary importance in his revolutionary development, while the dumber sufferings of a dependent laborer explain more of his temperament in 1792 or 1917 than the dialectics of the speeches he laboriously follows at the Jacobin assembly or in the Soviet garrisons of Petrograd.

In each instance, the historian must search into the experience of his subject to find the sources of his revolutionary consciousness. This is not an easy task, but it is a more approachable undertaking than the immensely broader one which addresses itself to determining the influence of any one writer or group of writers in a revolution. The historian can arrive at some relatively valid assessments of the effect of one or more writers on the consciousness of one revolutionary or even several revolutionaries. This is, of course, a very subjective activity and promises no statistical construct which will give us ultimately an objective analysis of Rousseau's or Montesquieu's presence in the French Revolution. But such presence is more likely to be found in subjective individual inquiries than in a broad counting of references in speeches and pamphlets. It is important to know that what Rousseau wrote made a difference in the consciousness of one revolutionary. That is what this essay intends to establish. That for the socialist revolutionary, Gracchus

3 Kingsley Martin, *The Rise of French Liberal Thought* (New York, 1954), p. 68.

Babeuf, in 1796, what Rousseau and Mably, and Abbé Morelly had written decades earlier was of crucial importance. Certainly much else was of importance to Babeuf in 1796, and this essay will not attempt to determine relative degrees of these contributing forces. It is enough to establish Babeuf's major intellectual debts.

Babeuf came to these writers unsystematically and informally by the avenue of self-education. He apparently was given a fair measure of pride by his father, a man of education and experience well above his later station in life. At his death, his father left his young family in penury, but he had already begun the education of Babeuf, his eldest son, in mathematics and had introduced him to classical literature. After a brief rebellious period, Babeuf began his apprenticeship as a *feudiste* and took up a dedicated interest in the conditions of man, particularly the poor. He read what was popular in the reform literature of his generation, most particularly from Rousseau, Mably, and Morelly, and from the beginning he was attracted to the most egalitarian ideas and to the most egalitarian reading in this literature.

We do not know specifically which of these most formative sources Babeuf had read with care and conviction before the Revolution. Our most valuable access to the prerevolutionary Babeuf exists in his complete correspondence with Dubois de Fosseux, corresponding secretary of the Academy of Arras.[4] For nearly three years he was on the secretary's crowded list of correspondents, sometimes engaging his individual attention. He gained access through this correspondence to a wider and more literary world. While he demonstrated an interest in literary criticism, his real concern lay with questions of social morality; the flow of the correspondence bears this out. The Academy, typical of its kind in the eighteenth century, gave some attention to social reform questions, but it was primarily involved in literary interests. In the nature of this correspondence, Babeuf had to answer countless questions on grammar and poetry, but his enthusiasm and interest are most apparent in his comments on social structure and property relationships in the Old Regime. In one letter in particular, written in July 1787, he set down a strong egalitarian response to a question on inheritance rights. For his part, the Secretary's reply to this serious argument was limited to a few lines, noting primarily the unrealistic idealism in Babeuf's appeal. By the autumn of 1787, Babeuf found the demands of the correspondence too shallow to justify the time it took from a busy and suddenly tragic life. In the spring of 1788 the correspondence died.[5]

4 The most nearly complete collection of this correspondence is to be found in the following edition: François-Noël Babeuf, *Correspondance de Babeuf avec l'Académie d'Arras (1785-1788)*, ed. Marcel Reinhard (Paris, 1961).
5 In two letters, dated September 6 and 7, 1787, Babeuf responded caustically and bitterly in reply to the shallow questions being asked and the time they took from his work and more serious interests. Dubois de Fosseux was incensed at such cheek from

In this correspondence, in some private notes associated with it, and in the introduction to his one published work on the eve of the Revolution, *Le Cadastre perpétuel*, we have the fullest expression of his social and political commitments as they had developed before he became caught up in a revolutionary career.[6] Most of this material reveals a young man with a profound empathy for people, and most particularly for the poor, the oppressed, and the dependent. It was no arid, isolated, egalitarian quirk. He was intensely humane, a loyal son and husband, a loving and attentive father. It was this open and sympathetic character which Babeuf brought to the writings of the eighteenth century, however unsystematically he read them. It is no surprise that he favored the expressions of egalitarian reform, not the bourgeois equality of competition, but the social democratic equality of condition. There is no attention to political representation but much attention to equality of well-being, of services, and of property. However, in only one piece does he reveal a collectivist commitment that is the substance of the later "Conspiracy of Equals." In some rather extensive notes apparently written only for himself, he explored the basic outlines of a collectivist agricultural society in which agricultural exploitation would be taken from the hands of individual peasants and given over to cadres of agricultural teams of twenty to fifty individuals on collective farms.[7]

With this one exception, what Babeuf had to say can generally be fitted within a kind of *partageux* philosophy which was present as a radical, popular economic philosophy in the Old Regime. Even in this, however, he was cautious, and in his most public statement on the eve of the Revolution, there is little expression of this radical attitude on

his rustic protégé, coming just at a time when the secretary was beginning to take more interest in him. His own bitterly ironic letter of September 20 marked his sharp change towards Babeuf. In the following eight months another ten letters were exchanged, but with the exception of Babeuf's moving, heartfelt reflections on the life and tragic death of his four-year old daughter in November, the subsequent letters were increasingly perfunctory. Babeuf, *Correspondance*, pp. 136-39, 141-42, 146-48.

6 The experience of Babeuf, growing up and working at his profession in Picardy, had an enormous influence in creating his fundamental egalitarian attitude. There are several essays which give attention to this experience. Lefebvre, *Etudes sur la Révolution*, 2d ed. (Paris, 1963), pp. 415-43; Antoine Pelletier, "Babeuf feudiste," *Annales historiques de la Révolution française* (hereafter cited as *AHRF*), 179 (1965), 29-65; Robert LeGrand, *Babeuf, ses idées, sa vie en Picardie* (Abbeville, 1961), and "Babeuf en Picardie," *AHRF*, 162 (1960), 458-70. See especially two recent studies: V. M. Daline, *Gracchus Babeuf à la veille et pendant la grande Révolution française: 1785-1794*, trans. from the Russian by J. Champenais (Moscow, 1976); and R. B. Rose, *Gracchus Babeuf* (Stanford, 1978).

7 V. M. Daline, "Les Idées sociales de Babeuf à la veille de Révolution," *Babeuf et les problèmes du babouvisme*, Colloque International de Stockholm (Paris, 1963), pp. 55-73. Daline bases much of his argument for Babeuf's prerevolutionary communism on a draft of a letter to Dubois which Daline believes was written in June, 1786. Babeuf never sent the letter which contains ideas on a collectivist organization of agricultural production, an idea which Babeuf never explicitly returned to.

private property. In the introduction of his lengthy technical manual on a permanent land survey and registration scheme which was published in the summer of 1789, he appealed to the National Assembly for a broad and generous social policy. In their concern for the poor and the oppressed, he pressed the Representatives to implement an immediate and complete reform in education. He insisted that the existing elitist educational system merely perpetuated an elitist and repressive society and that an educated citizenry is the only safeguard against social injustice.[8] Babeuf went beyond this appeal, however. He urged the deputies at Versailles to consider that society should seek to compensate for, not intensify, the natural inequalities in man. He suggested that the government might look at the arable lands in France which would average out at about eleven arpents (or something more than eleven acres) per household; by making such a division the deputies might well break the values and attitudes of an oppressive society. His *partageux* proposal, very cautiously offered as "remarks on an ideal order," was hopelessly out of step with the gathering bourgeois revolution.[9] It was only a matter of time before the young man with egalitarian inclinations and a strong populist spirit would find himself at odds with the propertied leadership of the Revolution.

He became involved, very soon, in an active revolutionary role which found him in constant confrontation with the established powers in his native Picardy and at the national level in Paris. It was inevitable, given his background and his sensibility, that he would become enlisted in the ranks of the extreme egalitarians. Abandoning at once his old career, he earned a meager existence for his family in the following years as a journalist and as an occasional public administrator. For the most part he championed at the municipal level, the district level, the department level, and at the national level a *sans-culotte* program of public welfare and popular franchise. He demonstrated a belief in the ultimate power of numbers, a citizen's army, a popular electorate, and an immediate surveillance through popular referendums and suspensive vetoes. He never relented in his attack on the prerogatives of private property; for Babeuf such rights were always subject to the superior responsibility of society in providing for the needs of all its members.

In this rigorous protest which he pressed in his newspapers, his correspondence, and in the public councils and committees on which he served, Babeuf demonstrated a thoroughgoing *sans-culottism*. He was constantly at odds with the moderate and propertied powers in the District of Montdidier and the Department of the Somme, and after they forced him to flee to Paris in 1793, he found work in the administration of the *sans-culotte* Commune of Paris. Although Babeuf spoke

8 Babeuf, *Textes choisis*, ed. Claude Mazauric (Paris, 1965), p. 100.
9 Ibid., p. 97.

no more of the agrarian law in Paris after 1793, he did not attenuate his social democratic demands, which found greater acceptance in the strong *sans-culotte* spirit of Paris. Perhaps the most rhetorical expression of his political-economic conviction in his early Paris exile came in a letter to Anaxagoras Chaumette immediately after the passage of the First Maximum in the National Convention.[10]

Most revealing in the letter is Babeuf's perception of the "needy" class which he defended, and his solution to their problems, which lay simply in an egalitarian distribution policy. Between his prerevolutionary theoretical egalitarian considerations and the later communism of the Conspiracy of Equals, this *sans-culottism* is the radical persistence in Babeuf's actions and expressed convictions. In typical revolutionary rhetorical fashion, he lauded Chaumette as the most conscientious leader in France who pushed towards the ultimate purpose of the Revolution, the organization of the will of the people in political action and the pursuit of their well-being through the state control of private property. Babeuf praised Chaumette for his work towards the "public welfare," the lifeblood of *sans-culottism* and the dominant theme in Babeuf's national vision. He did not speak of production when he wrote of public welfare; he sought it in a popularly-willed and state-directed distribution of goods. This was consistent with the "radical wisdom" of 1794, but by 1795 this wisdom was in retreat.

The laws of the *maximum* were repealed; a Thermidorean government abandoned the requisitioning and price-fixing tools of the Montagnard "economic terror"; prices soared, and national distribution channels dried up. The popular political response to this was defeated in the Germinal and Prairial insurrections in Paris; elsewhere the "little people" reverted to the traditional expedience of food riots and popular price-fixing. It is in this Thermidorian period, when the Revolution abandoned any serious social welfare pretense, that Babeuf freed himself from the politics and the sociology of the *sans-culottes* and returned to the more profound solutions in his earlier socialist thought.

After initial cooperation with the Thermidorians to return a free press to France, Babeuf had moved into opposition by October, 1794. In December he declared his willingness to assassinate any public official who threatened the institutions of popular sovereignty worked out in the Constitution of 1793.[11] This appeal he presented in his newspaper, which was enlisted in the propaganda to raise the urban masses to action again. After their defeats of 1795 and their desperate suffering in the inflation and shortages of a private commerce, Babeuf was forced into a thorough reappraisal of French social needs.

10 Ibid., pp. 152-58.
11 Babeuf, *Journal de la liberté de la presse* (Milan, 1966), p. 249.

His arrest in February, 1795, marked the beginning of the last chapter of his revolutionary career. While in prison at Arras during the summer of 1795, Babeuf's revolutionary experience and his earlier socialist idealism came together. His experience was of a mature revolutionary determined to carry an aborted Revolution to its just conclusions; his socialist idealism was revived by his perception of the Revolution in its Thermidorian period, the power of private property and the abandonment of what he thought a necessary reform direction. A letter to Charles Germain in July, dated one year to the day from Robespierre's execution, offered the first expression of this new conviction and this new determination.[12]

In this reply to a series of letters from Germain, Babeuf set down the basic outline of his subsequent political economic and social structure, "the essential ideas for our goal." He presented the justification for an unqualifiedly collectivist state. As he admitted to Germain, his ideas were yet incomplete, but the basic considerations were clear. The capitalist economy, which he identified as "commerce" as Mably had earlier, and which included all operations from the production of raw materials to the final distribution of finished goods, permitted a minority to oppress and exploit the majority. The key to the economy was in distribution, not production, and it determined the allocation and use of a very finite national product. As it was the key to a capitalistic society, so it was the key to an egalitarian society. Babeuf, borrowing from the pages of Morelly, saw the central institution of the plebeian society to be the national storehouse, not the national workshop. The administrators of these storehouses would gather the production of all Frenchmen and redistribute the goods according to need. The organization was not designed for maximizing production but for assuring an equal sharing of whatever was produced. His reply to Germain summed up eighteenth-century socialist thought.

What Babeuf added was the will for implementation. The letter to Germain did not present it; in this letter Babeuf was obviously rethinking his way back to a collectivist solution to the social problems of the aborted revolution for which he had sacrificed so much. When released from jail in the general amnesty of Vendémiaire, Babeuf returned to his newspaper and radically changed its format.[13] The *Tribun du peuple*

12 Babeuf, *Textes*, pp. 188-291.
13 The first thirty-two issues of his newspaper, *Le Tribun du peuple* which was entitled *Journal de la liberté de la presse* until issue number twenty-three, was printed in 338 pages. It became an inflammatory voice from the left, commenting on current events. The new format, beginning in November, 1795 was used in only nine issues before Babeuf's final arrest in May, 1796, yet it filled a total of 308 pages. It ceased to be a newspaper in the conventional sense, as Babeuf himself remarked that it was "a substantial work of mature thought and commentary and could not be measured by the inch or by the quarterhour in its delivery." In fact it became the organ of the conspiracy, calling the citizens to arm themselves and presenting the collectivist intentions of the new revolutionary future. Babeuf, *Le Tribun du peuple* (Milan, 1966), p. 147.

became the organ of the gathering conspiracy. Through it, Babeuf pursued two goals: to raise the revolutionary consciousness of a defeated and depressed popular force, and to explain and proselytize the collectivist society he and his colleagues would create in France., When he wrote to Germain in July, he cautioned him against impatience and warned that the "plebeians" in France were in no spirit to fight for the new society. At that time he contemplated a kind of Plebeian Vendée, which would win over France by example, not unlike Fourier's later utopian *phalanstère*.[14] By November in his "Manifeste des Plébéiens" he had abandoned the cautious utopian paths of his eighteenth-century socialist sources and had accepted revolution as the only possible avenue, concluding the Manifesto with the challenge:

> Things cannot get worse; they can only be improved by a complete overthrow!!! let confusion reign! . . . let all elements boil up, entangle, clash within, . . .let all enter into chaos and from that chaos, a new world will emerge, reborn.,[15]

But the economic proposition of the Manifesto was that of the earlier program suggested to Germain, and it changed little in its basic construction, in its subsequent public appeals, and in the private planning of Babeuf and his fellow conspirators. In its basic economic and social construction it remained tied to eighteenth-century socialist thought.

II

To be sure, much of the egalitarian thought of the eighteenth century which influenced the young populist and revolutionary stopped short of any collectivism. Even the *loi agraire*, which struck such fear in the hearts of the bourgeois revolutionaries that they made it a capital offense to propose it publicly, was simply a radical egalitarian expression of the dominant interest in land tenure of eighteenth-century agrarian reformers. Most reform literature in the century found the profound inequalities unacceptable in its national vision for France. Much of this literature contained a genuine concern for the impoverished and a considerable disgust with the rich. Such statements carried a socialistic flavor, and so appealed to the young Babeuf, but they lack an essential ingredient—the rejection of the institution of private property. Despite their egalitarian rhetoric, the writings of the *philosophes* never seriously questioned the inviolable nature of private property.

14 The term "Vendée Plébéien" appears repeatedly in Babeuf's writings; when he wrote to Germain in July, 1795 of "our Vendée," he spoke of isolated communities, separating themselves from the constitutional society of France, and by the very superiority of their collectivist system spreading wide, eventually to cover all France. Babeuf, *Textes*, p. 200.
15 Babeuf, *Le Tribun*, p. 107.

There were a few in the eighteenth century who rejected private property outright; they recognized the chimera in a *partageux* reform. This is expressed unequivocally in both Mably and Morelly. It appears fleetingly in Rousseau. There is no question that above all others, these three most directly shaped the thinking of the young Babeuf and gave articulate expression to the populist and the communalist nature of the young Picard feudiste.[16] We have Babeuf's own testimony at his trial at Vendôme when he charged these, more than any others, as having "corrupted" him to accept the values he held most dearly and would surrender only in death.[17]

The whole of the Conspiracy of Equals is not to be found in this "corruption"; but the moral argument, the rather primitive economics, and much of the political formula of a popular, collective society were extracted from the authors under question. In a general way, Rousseau provides the broadest political and social, even economic, background of Babouvism. Interpretations of Rousseau have always fluctuated between his emphasis upon the individual and his emphasis upon society. There is certainly present in his work material to arm those in either camp who praise or attack him for one or the other in his writing. Sounder interpretations have reduced the dichotomous nature of Rousseau's writings, by finding even in his most outspoken collectivist statements essentially a search for a social structure which did indeed promote the fulfillment of the individual rather than his prostration before an all-powerful state. However this debate is pursued, it is primarily of interest here to note that in the passionately argued political writings of Rousseau there is a strong appeal to the community and to a communal well-being. Of even greater importance, this appeal comes from a popular vision. Cobban reminds us of what Brunetière said of Rousseau, that he, unlike Voltaire, knew what was in the minds of the poor who suffered under the Old Regime.[18] There is a strong egalitarian flavor in Rousseau that in specific remarks and general themes impressed those in the late eighteenth century who had been poor and oppressed themselves, like Babeuf, or those like Buonarroti, who had developed a deep empathy for the *sans-culottes*. It is not so much that Rousseau persuaded these social democrats to some

16 I mean by "communalist" the combining and sharing qualities of life in rural Picardy where Babeuf grew up. The communal land tenure and agricultural habits of the Picard village were well known by Babeuf and prepared a readiness for an egalitarian solution. The reader can pursue this important aspect in the development of Babeuf's socialism in the works cited in footnote six above.

17 Victor Advielle, *Histoire de Gracchus Babeuf et du babouvisme* (Paris, 1884), II, 43. Babeuf's defense before the High Court of Vendôme is carried under separate pagination in the second volume of Advielle's study following Babeuf's correspondence with de Fosseux. For an English translation of the major parts of this defense, see Gracchus Babeuf, *The Defense of Gracchus Babeuf*, trans. and ed. John Anthony Scott (University of Massachusetts Press, 1967).

18 Alfred Cobban, *Rousseau and the Modern State* (Hamden, Connecticut, 1964), p. 135.

brand of a communal society, as that he gave the most enlightened expression of this theme and attitude in the eighteenth century.

There is as well in Rousseau, more purposefully stated than in most eighteenth-century writings, a strong egalitarian theme which bound the institution of private property with serious restrictions. It matters little that Rousseau was not at all a socialist, nor that he several times stressed the sacredness of the institution of private property. When he wrote in the "Discourse on Political Economy" that well-known passage decrying the first man who staked out a piece of property for his own and traced from this wilful act all subsequent social vices, Rousseau marked out private property for destruction in the eyes of Babeuf.[19] Further, Rousseau in several of his writings made a strong case against the inviolability of private property as a natural and inalienable right of the individual. When any possible conflict arises, society's needs overshadow the individual's rights. In the *Social Contract*, he wrote:

> For the state, in relation to its members, is master of all their goods by the social contract, which within the state, is the basis of all right. . . . However the acquisition [of property] be made, the right which the individual has to his own estate is always subordinate to the right which the community has over all.[20]

At about the same time, in *Emile*, he argued the logic of the collective spirit which resides in the spirit of the General Will:

> The State itself is founded on the right of Property. This right is inviolable and sacred for the State, so long as it remains private and individual. But directly as it is considered a right of all the citizens, it is subordinated to the general will, and the general will can annul it. The Sovereign has no right to touch the possessions of either one individual or several. But it has every right to appropriate the possessions of all.[21]

More specific and unqualified socialist thought was, of course, available to Babeuf, but nowhere was the core of a communal society so unsparingly and convincingly argued as in the concept of Rousseau's General Will. However mercurial this concept became in the hands of the interpreters of Rousseau, for Babeuf, and for all the popular leaders in the French Revolution, the concept became the living soul of a popular republic. Rousseau more than any other eighteenth-century voice wrestled with the problem of popular sovereignty, that is, the vesting of sovereignty in the great mass of people where passions held sway rather than in a small body of erudite men in whom reason played a greater role. Rousseau tried to reconcile the democratic dilemma of liberty and equality in making the body politic indivisible, in

19 Jean-Jacques Rousseau, "A Discourse on Political Economy," *The Social Contract and Discourses* (New York, 1950), pp. 234-35; Advielle, *Histoire*, II, 46.
20 Rousseau, *Social Contract*, pp. 19-20, 22.
21 C. E. Vaughan, *The Political Writings of Jean-Jacques Rousseau* (Cambridge, 1915), I, 108.

creating an all-pervasive egalitarian interest which would obviate any possible dichotomy between the rights of one individual and the interest of all individuals. He projected a separation of state (an executive of public servants or agents) and society (the legislature of the sovereign body politic), leaving the daily administrative routine to the former and formulating a General Will which directed and determined the interests and actions of the latter. He was primarily interested in a normative discussion of a society and politics organized on the sacred principle of the "general welfare." This principle, embodied in the Declaration of Rights of 1793, became the masthead of Babeuf's journal in the autmn of 1794, and the founding moral and social ideal of the socialist conspiracy in 1796.[22]

It is here that Rousseau had his greatest general influence within the ideology of Babeuf and his colleagues, the social spirit which all shared. While Babeuf came to this spirit independently of Rousseau, it is this spirit which inspired him to borrow deeply and single-mindedly from the communalism in Rousseau's writings. To be sure the "inspiration" created some distortion. When Babeuf found the "elixir" of the *Social Contract* in the formula, "In order for a society to be perfect it is necessary that each person has enough and that no one has too much," he both misquoted Rousseau and gave the statement a stronger egalitarian thrust than its original context justified.[23] Yet there is much that is there in Rousseau which confirmed the single-minded reading Babeuf gave it.

Still the Babouvists could not carry Rousseau with them to the final realization of the social, political, and economic implications they extracted from him. In the unreformed, libertarian society they saw in Year III of Republican France, the General Will was a chimera. The severe checks the popular revolution suffered in Years II and III gave ready evidence to the profound conflict of interests within society and the great advantages the propertied minority held in France in 1795-1796. Mazauric traces in this recognition the Babouvist abandonment of a Rousseauist, spontaneous popular Revolution and the movement towards the conspiracy by a revolutionary party, directing the overthrow of the entrenched minority and controlling affairs until the ideal society would be established.[24] Babeuf's sociology, his class

22 Babeuf, *Journal de la liberté de la presse*, no. 19.
23 Babeuf, *Le Tribun*, pp. 92-93. Mazauric notes that Babeuf cites this statement, which is taken from the closing footnote of Chapter 9 of Book 1 of the *Social Contract*, three times, and each time he distorts its meaning. Certainly Chapter 9 is far from an attack on private property, quite the contrary, in fact. His statement that "Laws are always of use to those who possess and harmful to those who have nothing: from which it follows that the social state is advantageous to men when all have something and none too much," was in reality an aside, but an aside which stuck in the mind of Babeuf and became for him the fundamental theme of the whole treatise. Babeuf, *Textes*, p. 210, n. 2.
24 Claude Mazauric, "Le Rousseauisme de Babeuf," *AHRF*, 34, no. 170 (1962), 464.

antagonism as it appears in his newspaper, is the somewhat simple
preindustrial confrontation of poor against rich.

> This war of the plebeians and the patricians or the rich and the poor does
> not exist only at the moment it is declared. It is perpetual. It begins at the
> moment when the institutions permit some to take possession of all,
> leaving nothing to others.[25]

While he continued to promote this confrontation in his newspaper in
1795 and 1796, Babeuf and his fellow conspirators had moved beyond
the spontaneity of such open confrontation, towards a revolutionary
elite which would direct, control, and organize the popular revolution.

Rousseau himself never faced the problem of implementation and
was profoundly pessimistic about any realization in France of his ideal
state. His stress upon a unitary society forced him away from any
concept of class warfare; he did recognize that at formative junctures in
history an individual legislator or a small group might, in fact, possess
an exclusive awareness of the General Will. But he was not really
concerned with the historical implementation of such insight, and
offered no such formula. Babeuf and his colleagues in the spring of
1796 were so concerned, and their strong Rousseauist commitments
made them ill-prepared to handle their terrible responsibility. They
fumbled with the problem of popular sovereignty and the necessary
corollary—unanimity in a popular revolution. Such unanimity despite
their appeals did not exist, and only reluctantly did the Babouvists turn
to the preparation for a temporary dictatorship. As Buonarroti expressed it, they "had almost decided, after having hesitated for a long time,
to ask of the people a decree by which the initiative and the execution of
the laws would be confided exclusively in them"[26]

They intended to create with these powers a society where the
General Will would not be confounded by the class antagonisms
created by property and competition. Authority would rest with the
people whose interests and will would become "general"through their
equal experience. Their agents would be the administrators for society
and their conduct would be watched and guided by a senate of elders.
Absolute equality would overcome the corrupting powers of vested
interests which Rousseau feared.

> The enlightened decisions of the people on general issues should be
> contrary to neither the equality nor the well-being of society, and they
> cannot be thus as long as equality exists in the full understanding of this
> word.[27]

All of this would begin within the initial popular revolutionary movement which would become the "national community" after the Revolution. This "national community" constituted the new society. Enroll-

25 Babeuf, *Le Tribun*, p. 13.
26 Philippe Buonarroti, *Conspiration pour l'égalité dite de Babeuf* (Paris, 1957), I, 153.
27 Ibid., p. 172.

ment appeared to be voluntary, but the conspirators would construct new social roles in such a way as to encourage membership and participation. No time schedule for its full development was established, but they anticipated nearly full participation within a short span of years. Until the new society was viable, however, the conspiratorial dictatorship intended to maintain its exceptional powers.[28] They were uncomfortable with such an exceptional state and planned much more enthusiastically for a post-revolutionary France where their goals were institutionalized and where force was replaced by voluntary participation and civic education. Again they found support and direction in their own reading of Rousseau.

> It is not enough to say to the citizens, *be good*; they must be taught to be so; and even the example, which is in this case the first lesson, is not the sole means to be employed; patriotism is the most efficacious. . . . The fatherland could not exist without liberty, nor liberty without virtue, nor virtue without citizens; create citizens, and you will have everything you need.[29]

Rousseau's patriotic education is quite separate from his ideas on a natural education, as he presented it in *Emile*. In fact, Babeuf had once found the latter interesting enough to consider for his own children, but the projects of the Conspiracy accepted unquestioningly the purposes and means of the patriotic education for the communal state. Perhaps the most pointed expression by Rousseau on such an education is from the passage cited above in which he pleaded the case for an education which emphasized fraternity over individualism and a public experience over a private one. Rousseau stated unequivocally that "public education . . . is one of the fundamental rules of popular government or legitimate government."[30]

Babeuf's interpretation of these Rousseauist ideas for a creative and formative education towards a communal society was evidenced throughout his writings. It was the formative experience for the young citizen which was the key to a collectivist democracy.[31] Conversely, Babeuf insisted that its monopoly was an essential tool in the class oppression of Thermidorian France.[32] He found this same emphasis upon a civic education in his other mentors. In fact the conviction is manifest in the reform literature of the eighteenth century.[33] Few

28 Ibid., pp. 220-23.
29 Rousseau, "Discourse on Political Economy," *Social Contract*, pp. 301, 307.
30 Ibid., p. 309.
31 Buonarroti, *Conspiration*, II, "Analyse de la doctrine de Babeuf," p. 105. "The Analyse" was a propaganda pamphlet which appears to be the most concise explanation of the doctrine of the conspiracy on the eve of its planned insurrection. A more complete expression of the educational plans for the new society is to be found in Buonarroti's recollections on pp. 201-209 in the same volume.
32 Babeuf, *Le Tribun*, pp. 104-105.
33 One can question along with Maurice Dommanget why Alfred Espinas would be surprised at the degree of attention to pedagogy in the conspiracy. Maurice Dommanget, "Babeuf et l'education," *AHRF*, 32, no. 162 (1960), 488.

writers, however, promoted these egalitarian ideas for education so eloquently and so convincingly as Rousseau. It was heady material for those becoming convinced of the necessity for equality within society and searching for the means of realizing and institutionalizing it. What the Babouvists then found in Rousseau was the most impassioned and reasoned statement of a social justice which emphasized above all else the equal right of all to live, and to live in as much ease as their society can achieve. He was not an exclusive source in any particular argument on education, or property, or economic organization, but he was the most persuasive and pervasive voice in the late eighteenth century for the egalitarian spirit which was a first stepping stone for Babouvism. When he wanted, Babeuf could take from these works pointed attacks upon what he saw as the basic faults of both the Old Regime and liberal societies—property and competition.

III

In turning to the works by Gabriel Bonnet de Mably, we find a more fundamental rejection of private property and persistent affirmations that the whole purpose of society could only be realized by a public organization and direction of the economy. Yet it was a moral charge to mankind, not a revolutionary call for change. At one point, he even warned against the implementation of his own appeal, confessing gloomily that "where property is established, it must be considered sacred and the foundation of society. To destroy it is a chimera, and the attempt will only bring greater troubles."[34] It was Mably's socialistic morality which was present in the early Babeuf, when he was still an idealist and not yet a revolutionary. It appeared directly and indirectly in Babeuf's writings well before his trial by the High Court at Vendôme. There Babeuf referred repeatedly to the communism in Mably who had prospered under the Capets but "would be sitting before the High Court in these days of liberty."[35]

Earlier, in his revealing letters to Abbé Coupé, in 1791, Babeuf reminded the newly elected Representative of the Department of the Somme of their mutual interest in Mably.[36] Stopping short of a full collectivist appeal, Babeuf spoke favorably of Mably's preference for a directed economy and an equal distribution of goods. Several years before this, Babeuf had discussed the moral charge of the new government in the "Discours préliminaire" of his Cadastre perpétuel which he had dedicated to the National Assembly in the summer of 1789. It was strongly Mableian in its moral tone, its metaphor of society as a large family, and the equality of rights and duties within it. Babeuf did

34 Gabriel Bonnot de Mably, Oeuvres complètes de l'abbé Mably (Paris, 1796), XIII, Principes de la législation, pp. 103-104.
35 Advielle, Histoire, II, 48-52 (the italics are Babeuf's).
36 Babeuf, Textes, pp. 145-46.

hint at a kind of solution in some equal land partitioning, but he gave no serious consideration to its implementation.[37] Of greater importance was the egalitarian conviction in this public "Discours" and in his private correspondence which is clearly based upon a generous moral persuasion more than on any rigorous economic or political argument.

When he returned to his earlier collectivist thought during his incarceration in Arras, the influence of Mably was manifest. Much of the communism in his letter to Charles Germain was closely related to the morality of Mably's *Principes de la législation*. Babeuf shared the limited economic perception of Mably, seeing production primarily in terms of distribution, and using the term "commerce" to signify the whole of the economic activity of society.[38] Like Mably, Babeuf identified the merchant as the directing force in the economy and, as the directing force, also the corrupting force. It is this perception, born of an agrarian-manufacturing society, which inspired each to concentrate his collectivist persuasion on distribution more than on production systems. Considering Babeuf's ready recognition of his indebtedness to Mably, both early and late in his public career, it is reasonable to conclude that this similarity came from Babeuf's use of Mably's socialistic morality which made sense to him.[39] Babeuf, however, was writing a generation later and witnessed a more industrial French economy than had Mably. Whereas the more profoundly agrarian and pessimistic Mably contemplated the languishing of arts and commerce, Babeuf denied the necessity or desirability of such a development.[40] Like Mably, he favored the disappearance of international trade, but Babeuf argued that a self-sufficient France within a socialist economy would see its arts and commerce in fact flourish.[41] However, the economic construction, the apparently parcellized agrarian and artisanal production, and the collectivization of distribution, are the same. The basic moral relationship binding this together—the responsibility of society for the well-being of the citizen, and the service owed by each citizen to society—this is the civic morality which is the substance of Mably's social philosophy and which is present throughout Babeuf's writings.

37 Ibid., pp. 98-99.
38 Babeuf explained to Germain that he used the word "commerce" to include the production of natural goods, the manufacturing of finished goods, and the distribution process. Ibid., p. 190.
39 This perception is clearly expressed in the discussion between the Swedish and English emissaries in Paris in which the simpler, less commercial Swedish society is shown to be decidedly superior to the commercial and competitive English society. Mably, *Oeuvres*, XIII, Books 1-2.
40 Ibid., pp. 127-30.
41 Babeuf, *Textes*, pp. 191-97. The famous "Manifeste des Egaux" drawn up by Sylvain Maréchal as the public manifesto of the conspiracy was never circulated on these very grounds. Maréchal stated forcefully that the "arts" could perish, if necessary, in the construction of a socialist system. The executive committee of the Conspiracy refused to support such a pronouncement. Buonarroti, *Conspiration*, I, 99.

Both Mably and Morelly operated from a fundamentally generous and sympathetic perception of man. For each, some social community promised man a better existence than living alone in the bush, as long as the community was organized in such a way as to promote and not restrict man's basically charitable nature. For each, as well, the noxious and unproductive characteristics of western societies in the eighteenth century could be traced ultimately to the institution of private property.[42] Unquestionably, Babeuf responded positively to this perception of man and to this assessment of the problem. From his correspondence with Dubois de Fosseux through his defense at Vendôme, Babeuf expressed this conviction, and he was from the beginning suspicious of private property. Morelly and Mably had articulated this moral and social framework in coherent and extended arguments which came into Babeuf's hands, thus influencing his ultimate political and economic conclusions.[43]

In his "Manifeste des plébéiens," in a sense the first public pronouncement of the Babouvist collectivist society, Babeuf twice repeated the maxim: "Discuss all you want the best form of government, you will accomplish nothing until you destroy the source of cupidity and ambition."[44] The admonition was clearly taken from Morelly, but it summoned up as well the moral attack Mably brought against private property as the source of avarice and ambition and competition, all of them destructive to the morally just society.[45]

For his part, Babeuf took from both, but went beyond either. Each was pessimistic about man's access to the collective society they both espoused. Ultimately, Morelly became more directly influential, in part because his pessimism was much less obtrusive and in part, because he put his moral conclusions into specific, utopian, collectivist form. Both Mably and Morelly were carried to their communism by a perception which separated them fundamentally from Rousseau. Neither argued that man came to a social agreement in order to protect his property. Morelly insisted that man responded to a moral attraction, while Mably

42 It is worth noting that Morelly on this very point took strong exception to Rousseau's first essay, "A Discourse on the Arts and Sciences," and the latter's rather facile condemnation of the arts and sciences as corrupting social man. Morelly, *Code de la nature*, ed. Gilbert Chinard (Paris, 1950), pp. 271-72.

43 It is simply not known when the works of Mably and Morelly came into Babeuf's hands, although there is evidence that he encountered Mably sometime before the Revolution, while in his correspondence with Dubois he came into contact with a somewhat fanciful form of Morelly's "Model of Legislation." Dubois from time to time between October 26,1796 and June 21, 1787 included excerpts from the prospectus of "l'Avant-coureur du changement du monde entier." Babeuf was singularly impressed with the egalitarian basis of this utopian prospectus and gave considerable attention to it in a letter of July 8, 1787, in which he declared himself irrevocably wedded to an egalitarian ideal, even recognizing that its realization would necessitate some kind of revolution. Babeuf, *Correspondance*, pp. 22ff., 109-12.

44 Babeuf, *Le Tribun*, pp. 93, 105.

45 Morelly, *Code*, p. 227; Mably, *Oeuvres*, XIII, Books 1-2, particularly pp. 43-45.

found the origins of society in man's growing awareness of, and need for, a moral community.[46] In either case, property had not pre-existed society and was not essential to it. Accepting this, their attack upon private property was less equivocal than Rousseau's. Rousseau insisted on the necessity of private property but subordinated its use to the large social good. Mably and Morelly each found that private property ultimately frustrated the purpose of society, the common welfare.

It is Morelly who offered in the eighteenth century the least ambivalent attack on private property, and it is Morelly who drew up a constitutional model for the new ideal society. Just once, in the opening statements to this model constitution which made up Part IV of the *Code de la nature*, did he express any pessimism concerning the access to the new society. He offered part IV, a "Model of Legislation," simply as an appendix to his relentlessly critical essay of the Old Regime "since it is unfortunately too true that it would be impossible, in our time, to form such a Republic."[47] This can be read as either the familiar pessimism of the utopian socialist surfacing in Morelly's treatise or simply as a prudent remark by a profound but circumspect critic of the Old Regime.[48] Whatever Morelly's purpose, the caution was ignored by Babeuf. In the spring and summer of 1795, he favored a voluntary avenue to the new society through the spread of model communes; by the autumn of that year, after his release from prison, he advocated an all-out class war to bring about its realization. In either case, Babeuf passed over the pessimism, perfunctory or profound, in Morelly and Mably and wrote unequivocally about the immediate realization of the new society.

The direct influence of Morelly, then, is more easily traced in Babeuf's fundamental ideas and, more important, in his proposed solutions; these were directly accessible to him without any necessary skirting around the reservations or ambivalence found in Mably and Rousseau. For Morelly the whole purpose of society was the realization of the general welfare.[49] The entire thrust of his philosophical argument carried to that conclusion. While he accepted a Lockean neutrality of human nature at birth, he argued that Nature conspired to prove to man the advantage of community.[50] Man's communal inspiration was to be found in a complex and mechanistic but beneficent universe, which created for man needs beyond his own individual capabilities,

46 Ibid., pp. 64-66. Morelly, *Code*, pp. 164-66.
47 Ibid., p. 286.
48 For understandable reasons, the most profound reformers of the eighteenth century were also the most pessimistic. Henry Vyverberg's *Historical Pessimism in the Eighteenth Century* (Cambridge, 1958) offers the most coherent explanation of this. Chinard suggests that Morelly's statement is more perfunctory than substantive. Certainly it stands as an isolated caution in an extended treatise which never reflects it in the other 174 pages. Morelly, *Code*, p. 283.
49 Ibid., p. 173.
50 Ibid., p. 165.

needs which encouraged him towards sociability. Sociability provided man with his fullest possible well-being, and ultimately sociability tied the well-being of one to the well-being of all.[51]

This sociability was not seen as inherent in man, but it was the organizing quality in man's most perfect social organization. To make it a voluntary behavioral pattern, society would have to make man appreciate the pursuit of his own self-preservation and well-being within a social relationship with his fellow citizens. This is the dichotomy of individual interests and a wide societal interest with which Rousseau wrestled. Mably, Morelly, and subsequently Babeuf, sought the solution primarily through a civic education which raised and reinforced communal identity and goals and which discouraged the development of individualistic and competitive values. The Babouvist sociology, expressed in Babeuf's writings and in the constituted plans of the conspiracy which were reconstructed by Buonarroti in 1828, as well as the sociology of their mentors, placed all stress on the rational powers of man and the ultimate logic of a collectivist society. An elitist educational system maintained a passive and disoriented population easily oppressed. Whereas a "plébéien" educational system was the key to a communal society structured in such a way as to relate the interests of each citizen entirely to a general well-being, its schools created a citizen who readily and with understanding worked within the laws of the community.

This interdependence of well-being, tied to an agrarian economy of a limited productive capacity, put emphasis upon distribution rather than production. Mably drew the most pessimistic conclusions from this perception, and when Babeuf is found making comments on frugality and mediocrity of supply, Mably's influence is more apparent than that of Morelly.[52] Yet it is this perception of a restricted production, quite at home in the eighteenth century, which inspired the stress these reformers placed on absolute equality. Babeuf, in his "Manifeste des Plébéiens," expressed what is at the heart of eighteenth-century communism in his warning that "no one can have too much without others having too little."[53] He echoed Mably's earlier argument against the chimera of near equality: "One cannot have any inequality of fortune without having both rich and poor."[54] Each in turn drew the same conclusion, that a socially controlled distribution of all goods produced by the members of that society was necessary to ensure an equal sharing of these goods.

51 Ibid., pp. 165-74.
52 Mably's dialogue between the Swedish and English representatives in Paris broadly pursues the ultimate abstemious proposition: "There is only one means to enrich yourself and that is to be content with mediocre fortune." Mably, *Oeuvres*, XIII, p. 134.
53 Babeuf, *Le Tribun*, p. 103.
54 Mably, *Oeuvres*, XIII, p. 45.

Before the Babouvist conspiracy, it was Morelly who most exactly worked out a legislative model for this society. His influence upon the ultimate Babouvist economic planning for the new society is unmistakable.[55] Babeuf had been favorably taken by such a model well before the Revolution, in a somewhat fanciful form. He and his colleagues approached it more seriously in 1796, as they made plans for a new France.

It is at this point that Babeuf and his colleagues went beyond their intellectual and moral sources. In 1795-1796, the revolutionary experience and frustration combined to force the Babouvists to break their idealistic bonds. There was developing in Babeuf's social, political, and economic construction of things, an ideology which promised not only a profoundly different ideal society for Frenchmen, but the makings of a transitional society which came from no utopian socialist. In its rawest form, it is written in anger and frustration and bitter rhetoric in the "Manifeste des plébéiens." In its most complete form, it is presented only thirty years later by Buonarroti who reconstructed the conspiratorial and constitutional plans of the conspiracy. In place of the rigorous uniformity of architecture and dress of the utopian egalitarian society of Morelly, the Babouvists offered the details for the confiscation and the sharing of the goods of a very un-uniform and un-equal society. The goal was a collectivist society, but there was recognition of the constitutional and material problems of moving the France of 1796 to the ideal society along a violent, revolutionary path.

This necessitated a society of its own, a transitional society of some indefinite duration. They were the first to see the necessity of a compromise society, in their case a dictatorship directed by the conspirators and their allies, to effect the new social and economic roles, and the new habits of obedience of the ideal, or goal society. Their conspiracy was hopeless, but this hopelessness detracts little from their historical role as the first modern proponents of a revolutionary communist ideology.

Yet in the formulations for the transfer and the egalitarian goal societies, Babeuf did not escape very far from his authorities. His revolutionary experience took him into the streets and made a political issue of what was primarily a moralistic one to that time. His political determination forced him to consider what to do with the towns and lands which existed, rather than to dream about another France of his own theoretical making. But his economic awareness is that of his authorities, i.e., oriented towards the distribution of the products of an agrarian and artisanal economy, not the organization of this produc-

55 R. N. C. Coe, "La Théorie morellienne et la pratique babouviste," *AHRF*, 30, no. 150 (1958), pp. 16-37. Coe compares the "Model" from Morelly's *Code de la nature* to the "Fragment d'un-décret économique"which Buonarroti includes in his history of the conspiracy. Despite the failure of Buonarroti to mention Morelly in any of his writings, Coe makes it quite evident that Morelly, while not the sole inspiration for the decree, is certainly the most significant source. Buonarroti, *Conspiration*, II,204-14.

tion. Before the Revolution Babeuf did explore briefly the collectivization of production, but he never returned to such a project.

Like his authorities, he worked out his collectivist intentions in
national granaries and public distribution. Both the national economic
proposal of Morelly and the proposed economic program of the conspiracy anticipated some collectivizing of agricultural production, but
the focus of each remained on distribution, not production.[56]

The originality of Babeuf is thus to be seen in the action he
brought to that collection of ideas and moral judgments put together
primarily from the sources cited, always taking the most progressively
egalitarian, the most optimistic interpretations of these sources. In a
very real way, these intellectual authorities shaped a mind instinctively
populist, and the sociology of the Babouvist conspiracy can be found in
their writings as interpreted by Babeuf. What mattered, of course, was
the mentality and the character of this interpretation. Babeuf was a
proud man, issuing from a singularly unusual father, a well-educated
but destitute and elderly man, who died when his son was still quite
young. He imparted to Babeuf ambition for learning and some important tools, but not an access to the secondary schools of France. Babeuf
then educated himself. While learning and working in a demanding
profession, he continued to read widely. Understandably within this
context and within the intellectual spirit of his world, he was dependent
upon authorities. His correspondence with the Arras Academy demonstrates a humility in the face of more learned men, but at the same
time, and this is of great importance, an uncompromising certainty in
his egalitarian instincts and a consuming interest in all ideas relating to
them, all ideas and writings which would give fuller articulation to
these instincts.

It would seem that an investigation of Babeuf's intellectual obliga-
tions rests on two fundamental questions. Why was he drawn to his
"authorities," and how did he use them? It is hoped that these two
questions have been considered and answered. To the degree that
Babeuf becomes an important actor in the Revolution and for subsequent socialist history, to that degree we see the historical effect of
Rousseau and Mably and Morelly at work.

Without their theories and their articulation, Babeuf remains a
disgruntled young activist, a committed family man, and perhaps a
modest local revolutionary in and around the towns of Roye and
Montdidier. Their writings provided a broader and more sophisticated
framework which shaped an egalitarian disquietude into a socialist
program. This is part of the link between historical fact and historical
action to which Lefebvre calls our attention. Between the historical fact
of the bourgeois revolution institutionalizing itself in the France of

56 Ibid.; Morelly, *Code*, pp. 287-93.

1795 and the historical action of the Conspiracy of Equals and its profound designs, a revolutionary socialist consciousness intervenes necessarily, and for this revolutionary socialist consciousness Babeuf is much dependent upon these mentors.

François Emmanuel Toulongeon: Contemporaneous Historian of the French Revolution

AGNES M. SMITH

Although it might seem proper that the study of the historiography of the great French Revolution of 1789 to 1799 should begin with the works of those who first attempted to write about it, little attention has been given to an analysis of the accounts of the Revolution that were published before the Restoration of the Bourbons in 1814. In fact, references to the earlier accounts indicate a consensus of opinion that the works produced in the years immediately after 1789 are not worthy of serious study; and there is an evident assumption that the pressure of events precluded a scientific approach by contemporary authors in their treatment of the subject. Yet a close examination of the *Histoire de France depuis la révolution de 1789* published between 1801 and 1806 by François Emmanuel Toulongeon reveals a remarkably intelligent attitude toward the task of writing history. And the inclusion of substantiating materials—documents, maps, charts, plans of campaign, and the like—imparts a scientific refinement to his presentation. A careful study of Toulongeon's approach to his task as well as of the work itself forces one to declare him at least an exception to the supposed "rule." His writing, like that of Thucydides, may cause the scholar to question the validity of the popular assumption of the inevitable weakness of contemporaneous historiography.

In 1881 the first volume of the review, *La Révolution française*, contained an article on historians of the Revolution which dismissed the efforts of the contemporaneous historians as of no value.[1] From that time through Pieter Geyl's and Alice Gérard's studies of historiography in the nineteen sixties, the writers of the era before the Restoration have been largely ignored or deprecated.[2] The well-known works

1 Albert Le Roy, "Les historiens de la Révolution," *La Révolution française*, 1 (1881), 257-75.
2 Pieter Geyl, *Encounters in History* (Cleveland and New York: The World Publishing Co., 1961), p. 95. Alice Gérard, *La Révolution française, mythes et interprétations (1789-1970)* (Paris: Flammarion, 1970). Gérard entitles her first chapter "Contemporary Passions and Eternal Debates," but she specifically excepts Toulongeon from her

on historiography by G. P. Gooch, Harry Elmer Barnes, and James Westfall Thompson all passed over the contemporary accounts of the French Revolution, and Lord Acton expressed suspicion of their worth, charging that the authors did not study history in "genuine and official sources."[3] Paul Farmer wrote that although the works of the contemporaneous authors "bore a historical character" they were of limited value either because they did not treat the Revolution as a whole or because they did not present a "consecutive narrative."[4]

A careful study of the subject of the writing produced during and immediately after the revolutionary decade reveals, however, that among the numerous authors who left information and impressions of contemporary events, there were several who set about to write serious histories of their time.[5] To dismiss these without even considering their merits seems inconsistent with the spirit of critical inquiry for the whole truth upon which the modern historian prides himself. It would seem that it is time to ask the question: Were there histories of any value prior to the Restoration?—and to turn to the sources to seek the answer.[6]

Among the many works, the only one dealing with the entire decade of the Revolution is Toulongeon's *Histoire*, which is also unique for its scientific approach. It is significant that the full title he gave to his four-volume study is: *Histoire de France depuis la révolution de 1789, écrit d'après les mémoirs et manuscrits contemporains, recueillis dans les dépôts civils et militaires.*[7] In appendices he reproduces letters, memoirs, maps, and other documents which he had found in those repositories and to which he refers in the body of his text. Published by Treuttel and Würtz in Paris, his *Histoire* is worthy of close examination as much for the information it contains on the Revolution as for the insight it gives into the character of the contemporaneous historiography of the time.[8]

general judgment of the first historians, that they have in common, "partisanship and the disdain for documents."

3 J. E. Acton, *Lectures on the French Revolution* (London: Macmillan and Co., 1910), p. 360.

4 Paul Farmer, *France Reviews Its Revolutionary Origins* (New York: Columbia University Press, 1944), p. 10.

5 Mary Agnes Monroe Smith, *The First Historians of the French Revolution* (unpublished doctoral dissertation, Department of History, Western Reserve University, 1966).

6 Alphonse Aulard, in one of his volumes of *Etudes et leçons sur la Révolution française*, made an important contribution to the study of this topic when he devoted three chapters to "Les Premiers Historiens de la Révolution française." From among the many possibilities he chose to write only on those "who were truly read, who truly exercised an influence"; and he found some fifteen such chroniclers of their times whom he thus designated as "historians." By drawing attention to these authors he has given other historians the opportunity to consider their works and to assess their relative value. Alphonse Aulard, *Etudes et leçons sur la Révolution française*, 9 vols. (Paris: Félix Alcan, 1910), vol. 6: chs. 2-4.

7 The word *dépôt* does not have an exact parallel in English. It refers to a depository for materials or archival collection limited to civil or military papers.

8 Toulongeon's *Histoire* was issued in both a four-volume and a seven-volume edition with the dates of issue for the four volumes, 1801-1806, and for the seven volumes, 1801-1810. Aulard's discussion of the publications of the first historians in his *Etudes*

The republican atmosphere of the early years of the first decade of the nineteenth century in France is reflected in the title pages of the first four volumes of the seven-volume edition; and two small, but noteworthy, omissions on the title pages of the last three volumes of the series indicate the shift in French political outlook away from republicanism, which occurred during the years in which this history was published. Volumes one and two are dated: "An IX—(1801)"; volumes three and four, "An XII—(1803)." All four designate the author as "Le citoyen F-Emmanuel Toulongeon." Beginning with the fifth volume, which was brought out in 1806, the designation "Le citoyen" is dropped, and the date of publication is no longer indicated in terms of the revolutionary calendar.

This work reveals throughout, the philosophical and vocational background of its author. Many years before the Revolution, François-Emmanuel Comte de Toulongeon had made a career in the army and had attained the rank of Colonel of Cavalry.[9] When Louis XVI summoned the Estates General in 1789 Toulongeon was elected as a deputy of the nobility from the *bailliage* of Aval in Franche-Comté.[10] He was among the first of the nobles to join the Third Estate in the National Constituent Assembly and was an active participant in the deliberations of that body from September 22, 1789 until his last recorded utterance on September 3, 1791.[11] His initial remarks reveal something of the liberal philosophical orientation credited to him by his biographers, for in the discussion of France's financial straits he said, "Luxury and sterile wealth will have to be sacrificed to save the country."[12]

He has been described as a lover of art and letters who was "impassioned by philosophical ideas and warmly received by Voltaire." Yet he was a moderate and while serving in the Assembly supported measures for the adoption of a Constitutional Monarchy.[13] He retired

---

et leçons described the four-volume issue and cited from it in the references. The seven-volume edition, available for use in the present study, is from the Andrew Dickson White collection of Cornell University. A later edition of Toulongeon's work was issued thirty years after his death under a different title but identical in its textual content. This edition of 1842, *Histoire de la Révolution française depuis l'ouverture des Etats-Généraux jusqu'à l'établissement du consulat*, has the same subtitle as the earlier edition pointing to the use of documents and contemporaneous manuscripts. It was published in Paris by J-P Aillaud in four volumes, quarto. In both editions the space devoted to the substantiating materials which the author termed *pièces justificatifes* is approximately one-fourth of the total; and in both, the materials presented are references for the textual content of the volume in which they are inserted. The four-volume edition of 1842, available to the present writer, is from the library of Case Western Reserve University.

9 *Nouvelle biographie générale*, 45: 529-31.
10 Claud Augé, *Nouveau Larousse* (Paris: Librairie Larousse), 7: 1067.
11 J. Madival and E. Laurent, *Archives parlementaires de 1787 à 1860*, 1st Series *1787-1799* (Paris, 1867), 9: 99; 42: 470.
12 Ibid., 9: 99.
13 Aulard, *Etudes*, 6: 110; *Nouvelle biographie générale*, 45: 529-31.

from political and military life at the time of the dissolution of the Constituent Assembly to spend his remaining years in research and writing. Going first to live on his family properties in Nivernais, he was found later among the émigrés who left France.[14] But the violence of the Revolution did not cause him to lose his sense of balance as it did so many others who wrote after 1793. With a perspective that is rare among contemporaneous authors, he wrote of the Revolution simply as, "the maturation of things."[15]

Explaining his philosophy of writing history, he said that every era has "a correct expression, a language, a style which is appropriate to it" and that an author "ought always to speak the genuine but contemporary language of the time that he describes." He concluded these remarks with the statement: "This observation is necessary in order that the historian not be accused of altering the system or (what could be worse) of creating a system in order to report there all the events and find there all the causes."[16]

His military orientation, revealed at numerous points in his remarks to the Assembly, is equally evident in his *Histoire*. In his Introduction he expressed the central assumption on which his treatment of the history of the Revolution is founded—the belief that political and military aspects of a nation's life are of equal import: "Military details must come abreast of domestic political events, for their influence has always been reciprocal."[17]

The application of "Reason" to the study of history which his era called for implied both objective reporting and a detached view of the subject matter. Furthermore, by both precept and example, Voltaire had introduced the concept of history as the record of man's total experience. All of these characteristics of historical writing are exemplified in the work Toulongeon produced.

Reflecting the emphasis on Nature so charactertistic of his day, he pointed out parallels between scientific and political developments: "Revolutions," he said, "are political crises as inevitable in the moral order of societies as are physical revolutions in the material arrangement of the universe."[18] Convinced of the importance of cause and effect in history, he indicated in his Preface that he believed it to be the function of the historian "to show people the causes of what transpires." But he saw the writing of history to be a service only if the treatment is impartial and if it is directed toward "showing all parties that the opposing parties are less odious than they believed them to be."[19]

14 Ibid.; Augé, *Nouveau Larousse*, 7: 1067.
15 F. E. Toulongeon, *Histoire de France depuis la Révolution de 1789*, 7 vols. (Paris and Strasbourg: Treuttel and Würtz, 1801), 1: 1.
16 Ibid., p. xv.
17 Ibid., pp. xii-xiii.
18 Ibid., p. 1.
19 Ibid., p. v.

Recognizing that it is generally thought to be hazardous to write the history of one's own time, Toulongeon noted that writing on a revolutionary period added to the difficulty. He believed, however, that these obstacles impeded only if one were partisan; and realizing the danger, he was especially careful to avoid the pitfalls of a biased approach. He considered himself to be in a position to write balanced history because philosophically he was between the Royalist and Jacobin view of the Revolution. Able to see both sides, he claimed he was not inclined to plead the cause of either, as his aim was to determine the truth. He wrote: "In revolution as in religion, only the factions are wrong."[20] He believed that the error of the partisans is to maintain and increase error if it reflects evil on their opponents. This they do, he wrote, "by always painting the other party in the blackest colors and by refusing to consider reasonably the interests and ideas of their opponents."[21]

Toulongeon believed that he had an advantage in writing in the first decade of the nineteenth century when:

> all the passions which served to produce the Revolution are less active or held in equilibrium by contrary forces, . . . a moment when emotions are less disposed to repress the language of reason and truth . . . the heart is tired of hatred . . . the arms are weary and the mind is precisely in that lassitude of prejudices that philosophers recommend for the search for truth.[22]

Beginning his study of the Revolution with a discussion of its causes, he dealt with many which have been emphasized by historians since his time. In a philosophical vein he wrote: "The revolutionary fires which the nations set ablaze have burned slowly for centuries and the moment of explosion is only that where the internal fire has come to the point of smaller outside resistance."[23] It is a curious point that although Toulongeon was greatly influenced personally by the *philosophes*, he did not emphasize their part in producing the Revolution—an influence which a few of his contemporaries recognized and which modern scholars believe to be of considerable significance.[24] Nor did he see in the agitation by the clubs and "thought societies" that propelling force toward the radical turn of the Revolution in 1793 which others have observed.[25]

20 Ibid., p. iii. It is evident that by factions Toulongeon meant extremists.
21 Ibid.
22 Ibid., pp. vii-viii.
23 Ibid., p. 2.
24 Crane Brinton, *Decade of Revolution 1789-1799* (New York and London: Harper and Bros., 1934), p. 6; Georges Lefebvre, *La Révolution française* (Paris: Presses Universitaires de France, 1951), p. 54; Philippe Sagnac, *La Révolution, 1789-1792*, vol. 1 in *Histoire de France contemporaine*, ed. Ernest Lavisse (Paris: Hachette, 1920), p. 75.
25 Brinton, *Decade*, pp. 18-20; Sagnac, *La Révolution*, pp. 229-31; Georges Pariset, *La Révolution 1792-1799*, vol. 2 in *Histoire de France contemporaine*, ed. Ernest Lavisse (Paris: Hachette, 1920), pp. 10, 88.

It is characteristic of him that although he himself had left France during the Revolution, he wrote regretfully of the country's loss through emigration and expressed his conviction that it was one of the great tragedies contributing to the instability of the French government.[26]

In writing of the leading figures of the era, Toulongeon presents well-balanced assessments of their character. He recognized and remarked upon the weaknesses of Louis XVI, and he noted that the King's vacillation was the despair of his friends and enemies alike.[27] Toulongeon saw a turning point in the relationship between the King and his supporters in Louis' failure on June 20, 1792, to veto the decree abolishing the King's Guard. He wrote that the King gave in too easily, disappointing the party that had supported him.[28] From that time on, says Toulongeon, the King's enemies had the upper hand.

Writing of Marie Antoinette, the author was much more sympathetic than other writers of his day or of more recent times as he described her personal character and told of her political intrigue. He noted, with understanding, that during the spring of 1792 the Court, under her influence, sought to have the Constitution altered to make it more aristocratic. In analyzing the charges which served as the basis of her trial he admitted that "they were very great" and acknowledged that "to the tribunal of posterity she was not innocent of all the offenses that were imputed to her." Admitting that she possessed "more imagination than judgment," he argued that one must be careful to consider that the state of revolution offered extenuating circumstances.[29]

His respect for traditional forms led Toulongeon to regret deeply the treatment accorded the Queen: "The civil hierarchy which the order of societies is obliged to admit, ought to be shocked to see the daughter of so many sovereigns, the widow of the last of so many kings go through the gate of a public prison to appear before a casual tribunal which was not competent for any citizen." He was appalled by "the vague and monstrous charges, the absurd and immoral denunciations" of her trial and he admired the "grandeur and true dignity" with which Marie Antoinette faced her accusers. His own belief was

26 Toulongeon, *Histoire*, 1: 81.
27 Ibid., 2: 72-73.
28 Ibid., p. 138. The King's Guard had been established in 1791 as provided in the Constitution of that year. In the debate over the second "Revolutionary Decree" in the National Assembly, Bazire, Guadet, Vergniaud, and Chabot argued for the abolition of the Guard. Supporters of the King who defended the retention of the Guard included Ramond, Dumas, Girardin, and Jaucourt. Others who are shown to have been strong supporters of the King at this time were Montmorin, Bertrand de Moleville, and the Parisian lawyer, Duport-Dutertre. Because the Guard was considered to be anti-revolutionary in sentiment, the decree was passed abolishing it May 29, 1792. The King assented to this decree reluctantly. John Hall Stewart, *A Documentary Survey of the French Revolution* (New York: The Macmillan Co., 1951), pp. 291-92.
29 Toulongeon, *Histoire*, 3: 104.

that "the public good which is doubtless a supreme law did not require
[such] a useless and barbarous sacrifice."[30]

Writing of the revolutionary figures tried and condemned by the
Convention, Toulongeon furnishes a balanced discussion of the accusations made by the radicals and of the defense presented by the moderate leaders. In his account of revolutionary activities he demonstrates
Lafayette's high military ability and his calm assurance of courage in
the face of public excitement. It shows how his arrival on a turbulent
scene would bring an end, if not to the disorder, at least to the excess.[31]
Toulongeon saw, however, that Lafayette lacked both "the defiance
and the force to avoid intrigues, and the skill to carry them through
when he found himself involved in them."[32] He believed that Lafayette
was motivated by the ambition for glory. "Fortune, honors, power were
for him only the means of a moment, and his character was not sound
enough to plan and carry through a political crime."[33] Yet the author
agreed with Lafayette in his criticism of the government and admired
his stand. Alarmed by the poor rapport between the army and the
Assembly, Lafayette wrote to the Legislative Assembly criticizing its
factional and intriguing spirit—especially the attitude of the Jacobins.
When they turned against him and Lafayette was forced to leave
France to save his life, Toulongeon's sympathies were entirely with the
once-popular general.[34]

Describing Robespierre as an astute judge of the political and
military situation in Europe in 1793, Toulongeon quoted from his
"Report on the State of the Republic" to demonstrate that it was, as he
said, "one of the most cleverly thought out and most artistically written"
reports of all those presented to the National Assembly in the autumn
of 1793.[35] Crediting him with having given an intelligent picture of the
political scene which evidenced genuine understanding of the situation, Toulongeon also remarked: "Robespierre had but one object—to
dominate by terror."[36] He sympathized with those who denounced the
radical leader for "paralyzing the will of the Assembly," and recorded
in considerable detail the attacks which brought about Robespierre's
downfall.[37]

In his treatment of the developments in national affairs Toulongeon expressed regret that France's pursuit of liberty led to the destruction of order both on the political front and in the army. He
observed that the weapon of the furor of the people employed in

30 Ibid., pp. 104-107.
31 Ibid., 1: 144.
32 Ibid., p. 89.
33 Ibid., p. 144. See Brinton, *Decade*, pp. 12-13; Lefebvre, *La Révolution française*, pp.
   136-38, for quite similar evaluations.
34 Toulongeon, *Histoire*, 2: 150-59; 203ff.
35 Ibid., 4: 145.
36 Ibid., p. 64.
37 Ibid., pp. 365-92.

lutions, "too often turned itself against even those who had intro-
:d the use of it; and the excess which wished to establish liberty was
____y surpassed by the excess which wished to destroy it."

Looking back on the activities of the National Constituent Assembly in which he had played an active part, he gave the details of the
deliberations over numerous laws and stated his conviction that its
management of government gained respect for that body both at home
and abroad.[38] In concluding his summary of the work of the Assembly's
committees he noted with approval that their political functions were to
have become the responsibility of various ministers under the new
government which they established by the Constitution of 1791.

Events were not to take the course intended by the Constituent
Assembly, however. With the advent of war during the period of the
Legislative Assembly, police power was soon granted to the Committee
of General Security, and Toulongeon noted that its assumption of
judicial functions over all matters from misdemeanors to high treason
created a sort of "inquisition." Continuing the simile, he wrote that
politics became something quite different from what he believed it
should be: "Crowd, drama, . . . tone, gesture, vehemence, reputation of
the orators produced in politics what the same measures had produced
in religion—fanatics, persecutors and martyrs."[39] Opposition was no
longer possible: "The Jacobins were masters of opinion and the crisis of
danger necessitated the rallying of all patriots to them, at least as long as
that state of crisis existed."[40]

After the initial panic the military situation soon improved.
Toulongeon wrote:

> Everywhere the Republican armies took the offensive. In less than thirty
> days after the 20th [of October, 1792] the allies gave up all the posts they
> had occupied on French territory. . . . All these events were concurrent
> with the first days of the French Republic and the first sessions of the new
> assembly of representatives of the nation which reunited under the name
> of the National Convention the legislative power, the exercise of all the
> executive powers and the distribution of all authority.

Yet as he saw it the situation worsened under the Convention government:

> No longer did they debate. Everyone felt obliged to vote under the danger
> of his life; each found his excuse in the weakness of others and his
> justification in the general subservience. . . . Stoicism was the only defense
> that they opposed to tyranny.[41]

In his account of the power struggle within the Convention, showing how the Mountain and especially the Committee of Public Safety
took over the reins of government, Toulongeon emphasized and de-

38 Ibid., 1: 182.
39 Ibid., 2: 143-44.
40 Ibid., p. 359.
41 Ibid., 3: 449.

monstrated the great power wielded by Marat. In his strong condemnation of the latter's brand of journalism he departed from his customary moderation. He referred to the unfortunate situation produced by
an "unbridled" press. Marat's *l'Ami du peuple* is cited as the worst
example of the mischief that can be perpetrated by an unscrupulous
editor in arousing the masses.[42] Both in the papers and in the clubs,
such leaders used the power of mass psychology "to the detriment of
law and order."

In great detail Toulongeon depicted the struggle between the
bourgeoisie and the *sans-culottes*. The accusations brought against
numerous leaders before the Tribune of the National Convention are
spelled out, and the influence of the Jacobin groups over the Paris
Commune is clearly portrayed. In describing the trial and acquittal of
Marat, the author showed clearly how the moderates were over-
whelmed.[43] In his view the Jacobins became virtually a political body in
the state. Certificates of Citizenship issued under powers of the revolutionary committees went only to people approved by the Jacobins
who thus exercised, "a general censure on the public authorities and
over all matters."[44] As Toulongeon saw it, Robespierre became all-
powerful because he was "master of the Committee of Public Safety
through the Jacobins."[45]

Toulongeon saw the war as the cause of the establishment of the
Terror, and he believed that there was justification for the Commune's
having assumed dictatorial powers in the crisis. Yet he regretted that
"terrible but voluntary servitude that each imposed upon all" to avoid
forced servitude to a foreign power. "They preferred the blade of the
executioner to the sword of despotic enemies," he wrote.[46] Because the
Terror solved the most immediate problem, its acts were sanctioned by
the people, and the Committee of Public Safety held the helm of
affairs, "with a harsh but unquestioned hand."

The generals of the armies were under the strict domination of the
government:

> The new French generals . . . carried to their armies the precise instruc-
> tions [of] the Committee of Public Safety. Success and victory was the first
> duty imposed. Reverses were misdemeanors which carried condemna-
> tion. Victory or Death was at the same time the instruction and the
> alternative that the government left to its favored generals. Even success
> did not always justify the others.[47]

And the success achieved by the military forces, whether because of or
despite this pressure, in turn enhanced the power of the committees

42 Ibid., p. 438; 1: 153.
43 Ibid., pp. 343-51.
44 Ibid., 4: 58.
45 Ibid., p. 300.
46 Ibid., pp. 91-92.
47 Ibid., p. 220.

and the club. Shortly, "Germany for a second time feared for her frontiers; those of France were entirely safe." He believed that at that point the government of the Republic had an assured position. And because he saw this to be the case, the events of January, 1793 came as a disillusionment for Toulongeon: "Terror within was no longer a necessary medium, and what proves that it was a prescribed method is that then it coldly employed all its rage."[48]

His viewpoint in this instance seems to have been conditioned by the fact that he thought only in terms of the dangers of foreign war. When the outside invasion of 1792 was repelled he felt the real emergency justifying the exercise of terror was ended. Perhaps it was his pride in the French military tradition that clouded his judgment, for he assumed that the foreign war was won when it was not. Furthermore, in thinking of defense of the frontiers as the only real crisis facing the leaders of the new Republic, he did not take seriously enough either the uprising in the Vendée or the Federalist Revolt, the continued threat of the British fleet, or the internal economic crisis. Those who opposed Robespierre, however, were determined that the Reign of Terror must be terminated; the end came in the political reaction of 9-10 Thermidor (July 27-28, 1794). Interpreting these events Toulongeon wrote that it was with great skill that the Revolution was slowed down in such a way as to "preserve the machinery that it might not be destroyed by the rapidity of the movement." What he had been longing for himself in national affairs had occurred.[49]

In the establishment of the Directory, however, Toulongeon saw no real improvement in the political situation within France. He wrote that she could still call herself a republic because the responsibilities of the three branches of government were separated on paper; but "the torrent of absolute power had exceeded all limits; tyranny reigned on the debris of the social edifice which it came to overturn," because a triumvirate of three directors continually nullified the minority action of the more moderate two.[50] In his discussion of the cause of the weakness of the Directory he suggested that the basic problem was that, "They had forgotten that in choosing men of opposing parties and characters the balances, to act usefully, must tend to a common objective." The trouble lay in the fact that: "The interests of parties are more active than the public interest."[51]

Toulongeon realized that the government had come to fear the army, and he was incapable of comprehending or sympathizing with

48 Ibid., p. 227.
49 Ibid., p. 364.
50 Brinton presents a more favorable picture of the accomplishments of the period of the Directory and demonstrates that the government was well on its way to achieving stability. Brinton, *Decade*, pp. 212-21. Another work which gives the Directory a favorable review on the whole is Lefebvre, *La Révolution française*, pp. 451-532.
51 Toulongeon, *Histoire*, 6: 2.

that attitude. He saw the debate over the proposal of peace with Austria in April, 1797 as a conspiracy to hold the military power in abeyance and keep it at a distance. To him it was incongruous, and he wrote: "It was perhaps the first time that one sees the generals of victorious armies desire to seek peace and the civil magistrates turn away from the means of it and postpone the end."[52]

The first historian of the French Revolution to give emphasis to its military aspects, he also offered insight into the relationship between military and political matters. Well aware of both the strengths and the weaknesses of France's old military establishment in which he had served under the monarchy, he was highly critical of the system by which only nobles could become officers, and he pointed out that this situation had made it easy to detach the army from its chiefs. He rejoiced when the time came that the quality of the army and the morale of the soldiers were improved markedly by the conviction that they were fighting for a cause which was truly their own. For historians interested in the tactical maneuvers of the "foreign war" Toulongeon affords many details of major engagements from the annexation of Avignon before the war to the account of the Egyptian campaign at the end. The military charts and maps add immeasurably to the value of such a presentation.

He attributed much of the early military weakness of the armed forces of the Republic to the excessive power of the clubs and the spirit of liberty which had made discipline within the army hard to maintain.[53] Characterizing the relations between the army and the Executive power as "uncertain and disorderly," Toulongeon wrote: "Such was the situation with the armies that their organization was hardly known and controlled." He cited a letter from Dumouriez to the President of the Legislative Assembly which began, "Not knowing whether there is a minister of war. . . ."[54] In this chaotic system there was no established hierarchy of command among the generals: they were constantly subjected to review and threatened with summary dismissal by powerful elements in the government who knew little about military matters. After the Convention Government came into being, the Robespierre group within the Jacobins began to fear Dumouriez's power and popularity as he continued to win battles, and his closeness to the Girondins made him even more the object of attack from the partisans of Robespierre.[55]

When Dumouriez wrote to the Convention Government on March 12, 1793 criticizing the Jacobins for interfering with army af-

52 Ibid., p. 188.
53 Brinton says that the application of the principles of Liberty, Equality, and Fraternity to the old professional army had disrupted it. Many of its officers had emigrated and those who stayed behind were distrusted by their men. Brinton, *Decade*, p. 58.
54 Toulongeon, *Histoire*, 2: 203.
55 Ibid., 3, 52, 297; cf. Sagnac, *La Révolution*, p. 350.

fairs, this letter turned powerful forces against him. But Toulongeon
noted that Dumouriez's letter painted a picture which, unfortunately,
was "too true."[56] The author's military orientation led him to agree with
Dumouriez in his criticism of the government's attitude toward its
armed forces; and he did not interpret the letter of March 12 as a
serious threat in the way the Convention did, probably because he
believed that France's interest would best be served by putting down
the elements that had taken control. Though not strictly objective at
this point in his narrative, he offers a useful interpretation of affairs.
Like the Girondins of his day, and like many other historians since, he
was transferred by the turn of affairs to the conservative position in
relation to the new spectrum of opinion.

Following Voltaire and the spirit of the age, Toulongeon enriched
his work by covering aspects of the life of France in matters other than
the political and military. Because of the special developments in religion associated with the Revolution, that topic is one with which all
authors of the history of the period have had to deal. But it was rare for
authors of his time to include in their accounts references to the
educational system, the theater, the arts, science, and literature.

The skepticism concerning religious matters which characterized
the Age of Reason is evident in Toulongeon's writing. Commenting on
the "pretended visions" of a woman named Catherine Théot whose
mystical experiences created some excitement at the time, he concluded that the mind of his day was not so credulous as to be taken in by
that sort of thing.[57] A clue to his own agnosticism is given occasionally,
as in the phrase introducing his discussion of the war at Avignon: "If
there is a Superior Providence who deigns to lower his glance. . . ."

The author has respect for the Church, however, and his account
shows that he was committed to religious liberty, with equality for all
faiths including Catholicism.[58] In describing the legislative session
which debated the Civil Constitution of the Clergy he showed high
regard for some of the nonjuring priests. As he saw it, the National
Constituent Assembly planned to neutralize the power of the clergy by
dividing them, but succeeded rather in bringing about persecution and
producing martyrs.[59]

Fearing any power that would compete with it in the minds of the
people, the Paris Commune moved in the fall of 1793 to replace
religion with the worship of Reason and the Nation. Toulongeon
presented the details of the instigation of the worship of Reason and
the establishment of the Temple of Reason. He wrote of the Convention with some irony that: "While the blood flowed around them they

56 Toulongeon, *Histoire*, 3: 292-93; 4: 220.
57 Ibid., 4: 347.
58 Ibid., p. 345.
59 Ibid., 1: 263.

occupied themselves with the institution of a new religion."[60] Discouraging the dechristianization crusade, the government soon decreed the principle of the existence of a Supreme Being and of the immortality of the Soul, which Toulongeon saw as a bid for popular favor. But in picturing the Festival of the Supreme Being he showed no enthusiasm for the fête.[61] He believed that people attended only because they were afrad not to, and that the festival had no effect on their thinking whatever. He wrote that all outward religion ceased in France and all education ended with it.[62]

Concerning artistic expression during the period of the Convention, Toulongeon noted that, "The Théâtre Français was closed. The masterpieces of Corneille spoke of a republican dignity, of an elevation of soul, of a Roman grandeur, of a public liberty which contrasted too much with the tyranny and oppression in France."[63] The plays that were produced and the language of the period continued to take the tone and the accent of the customs of the time. With the change in the character of the national spirit there was little development of the arts. There was music inspired by the war, but he claimed that the country went many years without producing a notable work of literature or science.[64]

Relative to economic matters, the author showed his acquaintance with the theories of Adam Smith in England who, he wrote, had "examined thoroughly" the causes of the wealth of nations. Toulongeon found himself, however, more in accord with the French physiocrats who based their precepts on what he termed the "true principle" that wealth comes from land and its products.[65] He also developed quite fully the story of the *assignats*, noting perceptively that one of the most remarkable phenomena of the Revolution was the way in which the illusion of "magic economics" of the "inexhaustible mine of the *assignats*" was sustained for seven years.[66]

With much of the activity of the French government centered on the "foreign war" in the latter part of the revolutionary era, Toulongeon's writing is frequently devoted to a treatment of foreign affairs. The activities of the *émigrés* are only part of the story. All through his account he referred to the general diplomatic situation in Europe and related the developments in France to the over-all picture. He also discussed relations between France and her colonies, returning fre-

60 Ibid., 4: 345.
61 Ibid., pp. 349ff.
62 Ibid., p. 124.
63 Ibid., p. 59.
64 Ibid., 5: 396-400. His assertion that there was little development in the arts to record is borne out by modern scholars, who would, however, point to the work of David in painting which Toulongeon failed to mention. Brinton, *Decade*, pp. 272ff; Lefebvre, *La Révolution française*, pp. 542, 556, 569-71, 577-81.
65 Toulongeon, *Histoire*, 1: 250ff.
66 Ibid., 3: 248.

quently to deal with affairs in Santo Domingo and the repercussions there of the acts freeing the Blacks.

In his final volumes, when Toulongeon shows the Revolutionary Epoch turning into the Napoleonic Era, a combination of circumstances hampered his usual "calm philosophic approach"[67] to the history of his country. He evidenced great hostility toward the Directory, and his weariness with war and internal conflict led him—as it led Frenchmen generally—to welcome the man on horseback. For Toulongeon it was perhaps his proclivity toward things military that was primarily responsible for his over-optimism regarding the prospects of the new era. In numerous passages throughout the sixth and seventh volumes he sang the praises of Napoleon and quoted at length from his speeches as proof of his high motives.[68] The history ends with the arrival of Napoleon in France after the Egyptian campaign, and Toulongeon's conclusion depicts high enthusiasm among the French people for the general who had enjoyed great success in most areas of the war.

Although Toulongeon did not maintain his dispassionate and objective view of French history into the Napoleonic era, his treatment of the earlier part of the revolutionary decade is a remarkable example of good historical writing. The charge that the contemporaneous writers were invariably biased, did not use documents, or did not treat the Revolution as a whole can fairly be made of most of the writers of the period, but these criticisms are hardly descriptive of the work of François Emmanuel Toulongeon. His intellectual commitment and stoical frame of mind helped him to achieve a balanced attitude toward the turbulent time such as no other French historian of the revolutionary era displayed.

In striking contrast to some of his contemporaries like François Pagès and Louis Prudhomme who emphasized atrocities in their special pleading against the Revolution,[69] Toulongeon deliberately refrained from submerging his account in blood. Discussing the insurrection of the Midi, he said: "The details and the enumeration of the deplorable excesses, set down in the accounts, leave monuments that history is not obliged to record." Writing of the war in the Vendée, he expressed the conviction that, "The historian is often obliged to avoid the circumstantial detailing of the horrors of which humanity ought only to preserve the memory as a preventative." He went on to make

67 This is the characterization of Toulongeon's work by Leo Gershoy.
68 Toulongeon, *Histoire*, 7: 43-46. The speech to his troops at the conclusion of the Italian campaign is cited here, pp. 43-46; the speech to the people of Tyrol claiming the objective of a peaceful Europe, p. 73; and a letter to Prince Charles pleading for peace, pp. 178-80.
69 See François Pagès, *Histoire sécrète de la Révolution française*, 2 vols. (Paris: H. J. Jansen, An V-1797). Also a seven-volume edition by Dentu in 1800. Louis Prudhomme, *Histoire générale des crimes commis pendant la Révolution française*, 6 vols. (Paris: Rue des Marais, An V-1797).

the general observation: "It is not necessary always to show men, as is possible, all that of which they have been capable. Forgetfulness demands its part of public crimes. It is the refuge that superior wisdom has allowed them."[70]

Toulongeon's willingness to accept change as inevitable is one of the characteristics that distinguishes him from lesser writers of his time. In his judicious interpretation of the controversial issues with which he dealt, his realization of the value of supporting evidence and the use of footnote references to the numerous documents inserted at the end of the volumes, this author offers an example of successful application of the historical method of writing of the history of events in which he was involved. It singles him out as a scientific historian decades before the scientific approach to historical writing was popularly advocated. His *Histoire* is ample evidence of the truth of his assertion that it was possible to write a balanced and relatively accurate account of the revolutionary era. It seems strange that it would be more than a century before French historians would again find themselves able to do as well.

70 Toulongeon, *Histoire*, 3: 358.

The Ardent Historian of an Ardent History: Albert Mathiez

JAMES FRIGUGLIETTI

When Napoleon declared that the French Revolution was "over," he referred to the events of 1789-1799, not to their interpretation. Since the coup of 18 Brumaire, each new generation of Frenchmen has sought to explain the causes, development, and consequences of that tumultuous period in terms of its own time and political outlook. The historiography of the Revolution has been undertaken by several writers,[1] but none has investigated in depth the career of one of the major historians, Albert Mathiez (1874-1932). His prolific output, ardent enthusiasm for the Revolution, and meteoric career are in themselves fascinating. But his life also reflects the concerns of the generation that came to maturity after the establishment of the Third Republic, which claimed the Revolution as its forebear and refought its battles both in textbooks and in the streets.

Albert Mathiez was born on January 10, 1874, at Fouillies-des-Oreilles, in the canton of La Bruyère, Department of Haute-Saône, to a family of small peasant proprietors.[2] To a considerable degree the basic personality and outlook of the man were determined by the place, date, and circumstances of his birth. These factors formed the center of his character. His education, historical training, political ideas, and polemics were accretions on them, taking the shape and peculiarities of his origins.

To begin with, Mathiez was a Franc-Comtois. In his physique and speech he remained one all his life. His friend Paul Mantoux described him thus:

> His massive torso, which seemed to have been shaped by the hard labor of twenty peasant generations, was that of an Atlas capable of bearing the

---

1 For discussions of the historiography of the French Revolution and brief analyses of the work of Mathiez, see Paul Farmer, *France Reviews Its Revolutionary Origins* (New York, 1944); Pieter Geyl, "French Historians for and against the Revolution," in *Encounters in History* (Cleveland and New York, 1961), pp. 87-142; Alice Gérard, *La Révolution française: Mythes et interprétations, 1789-1970* (Paris, 1970); Jacques Godechot, *Un Jury pour la Révolution* (Paris, 1974).

2 Full biographical details can be found in James Friguglietti, *Albert Mathiez, Historien révolutionnaire (1874-1932)* (Paris, 1974).

world on his square shoulders. His wide forehead and uplifted head, his pale blond hair and blue eyes with their direct gaze . . . made one think of the ancient Alamanni and Burgundians who invaded his native Franche-Comté.[3]

His speech was always to be marked by the rolled "r's" of the local dialect, and he retained a taste for the cuisine of his province.[4]

The family name, a form of "Mathieu" (Matthew), was common in the region of Luxeuil, where Mathiez's ancestors lived for generations. Before the Revolution, they were peasants who worked the land of the abbey of Luxeuil, which was under the control of the noble Clermont-Tonnerre family. The same year that the last abbé-seigneur acceded to the commendam, 1743, also marks the date for which we have the first definite information about the Mathiez family: the marriage of Claude-Louis Mathyer to Marie-Françoise Couberand at Luxeuil-Saint-Saveur.[5]

Claude-Louis was literate, for he signed the parish register in a firm hand. But like the other peasants in the area, he lived under the confining terms of the landlord's traditional authority. Tied to the land, the peasants could not settle elsewhere without the express consent of the abbot. An enlightened man, Clermont-Tonnerre had begun to abolish serfdom on his estates in 1782, although at a high price. Only the Revolution of 1789, which saw a peasant uprising against him at Luxeuil, completed the process of emancipation.

The son of Claude-Louis, Jean-François, born in 1755, lived through the Revolution, dying in 1807. His son, also named Jean-François, was born in 1780 and may have fought in the Revolutionary and Napoleonic wars. But in any event he died in his native region in 1855. By his marriage to Josephe-Gabriel Menigoz, he had three sons. The youngest, Claude-François, born in 1820 at Esboz-Brest, a few kilometers east of Luxeuil, married Marie-Françoise-Appoline Cheval-ley, the daughter of small cultivators from the area. The couple settled on the isolated farm of Fouillies-des-Oreilles, which belonged to the bride's father. Three children were born to them: Sylvestre-Emile in 1845, Constant-Aristide-Eugène (father of Albert Mathiez) in 1849, and Marie-Augustine-Sylvie in 1864.[6]

From military records we know that the two sons received schooling, but they remained cultivators on their father's farm. Probably

3 Paul Mantoux, "Albert Mathiez," *Annuaire de l'association amicale de secours des anciens élèves de l'Ecole Normale Supérieure* (1933), p. 88.
4 See Friguglietti, *Albert Mathiez*, pp. 192-228.
5 Archives Départmentales, Haute-Saône, Luxeuil, 311 E. Supplement v. Register of marriages and burials, vol. 49, v°.
6 Archives Départementales, Haute-Saône, Luxeuil, 311 E. Supplement K. Register of births, marriages, and deaths (1737-1758), fol. 118, v°; Supplement Y. Register of births, marriages, and deaths (1774-1780), fol. 235, v°; Etat civil, Esboz-Brest (1802-1813, 1813-1822), La Bruyère (1843-1852, 1863-1872); 103 E. Supplement 5, Censuses of 1841, 1846, La Bruyère.

nothing distinguished them from other rural families, and they no doubt continued to work the fields as their forefathers had done. The outbreak of the Franco-Prussian War in 1870 destroyed the calm of the region, however. German troops invaded Franche-Comté, clashing with republican troops at Villersexel in January, 1871. Sylvestre-Emile, who as a sergeant-major in the 85th regiment of infantry, fought in the war, died on February 16, either from wounds or from illness contracted while in service. Grieved at his son's death, Claude-François also passed away two months later.[7]

Two weeks before his death, Claude-François had drawn up his will dividing the family property between his two surviving children. Its provisions reveal the modest condition of the Mathiez family. Most important was a small stone farm house (which still stands) and fields totalling some 6 hectares, 24 ares (about 15 acres), divided into three plots, with an annual income of 350 francs. The household furnishings and tools were worth 1,400 francs. Debts totalled some 3,500 francs, including 1,800 owed to Constant. The family's livestock consisted of "two bulls, one cow and one calf"; their implements, "two scythes, two flails, a large hatchet, a hand ax, and a small saw." Domestic furniture included "two cupboards made of oak, a sideboard, three buckets, three pails, a churn made of pine with a cover, fifteen basins, fifteen faience plates, eight glasses, six empty demi-johns, a tin bottle, two lamps, three bottles—value estimated at 90 francs."[8]

At his father's death, Constant Mathiez became head of the family. Aided by his widowed mother and younger sister, he continued to work the farm. Perhaps to ease his loneliness, he married in March, 1873, Delphine Thiébaud, a girl of twenty-two, daughter of small farmers who lived nearby. It was on January 10, 1874, at 5 p. m. that a son was born to them. They named him Albert-Xavier-Emile.[9]

Nothing in his ancestry or background indicated that the child would rise in the world. The son of a small landowner who had difficulty making a living from his farm, young Albert was endowed with neither wealth nor social status. It is probable that neither of his parents had ever left the confines of Franche-Comté.

From his peasant parentage and rural background, Mathiez inherited certain qualities which would always mark him: his great physical strength, his capacity for hard work, and his stubborn independence. Spending his early years in the countryside, he grew up among the fields and woods, playing outdoors in the hot summers, and warming himself beside the fireplace during the long, cold winters. Mathiez later recalled how, when wolves howled in the woods that surrounded his

7 Archives Départementales, Haute-Saône, Etat civil, La Bruyère (1863-1872).
8 Notarial archives, Faucogney (Haute-Saône). Last will and testament of Claude-François Mathiez, dated April 2, 1871.
9 Town records, La Bruyère (Haute-Saône). Birth certificate of Albert-Xavier-Emile Mathiez, dated January 10, 1874.

rural home, his grandmother would hurl burning brands at them so that he might sleep undisturbed.[10]

The peasants of Haute-Saône were independent landowners who produced virtually everything they needed in the way of food and clothing, including their wooden shoes. But they had to work hard to secure a living from their small plots and grudging soil. According to an eighteenth-century writer, they worked "a sterile, cold, ungrateful and desolate soil, which scarcely returns to them the efforts of their seed, cultivation and manure."[11]

This harsh life impressed itself early on the young Mathiez. He always remembered hearing his grandmother recall how in 1818, "grain was so scarce and expensive that a quarter field was sold to obtain a bushel of grain."[12] Yet Mathiez was not ashamed of his rural ancestors. On the contrary, he could declare, many years after he had left the countryside, that:

> I am proud to belong, through numerous generations of peasants, to Franche-Comté, which has always practiced the great virtues of our race: hard work, a passion for independence, a frankness that verges on rudeness, good common sense mixed with shrewd insight, and a curiosity which sometimes pushes the mind to daring speculation. My province is as dear to me as my country.[13]

Mathiez's family was destined not to remain on the land, however. Like so many other peasants, Constant found it difficult to make a living from the soil. While retaining ownership of his farm, he moved to a nearby village where he opened an inn about 1876. A few years later he moved again, this time to the larger town of Lure. There he established himself as an innkeeper, operating an establishment with the aid of his wife and mother. Not long afterward, in 1885, a second child, a daughter, was born to the couple. Within three years the couple quarrelled, and Madame Mathiez left her husband, divorced him, and soon emigrated to the United States with her small daughter. For his part, Constant, along with his aged mother, settled in the small village of Saint-Germain, to the north of Lure, where he opened a cabaret, remarried, and died in 1909 at the age of fifty-nine.[14]

Because no personal letters or other substantial documentation concerning the family has survived, we can only speculate that the breakup of the Mathiez family left its mark on young Albert's personality. His own angry temperament and suspiciousness, his harshness in

10 Information given to the author by Mme Albert Lautman, step-daughter of Mathiez.
11 L. Barbedette, "La Terre de Luxeuil à la veille de la Révolution," *Annales historiques de la Révolution française*, 4 (1927), 159.
12 "La Famine dans l'histoire," *L'Internationale*, August 14, 1921.
13 "La Corruption parlementaire sous la Terreur," *Annales révolutionnaires*, 5 (1912), 157.
14 Archives Départementales, Haute-Saône. 103 E. Suppl. 5. Censuses of 1872, 1876, 1881, La Bruyère; Town records, Lure (Haute-Saône) (1885, 1903-1913).

dealing with opponents, and his resentment of superior authority no doubt stem from these years of childhood and adolescence.

Yet positive traits were also ingrained in him. Not only the traditional independence and tenacity associated with all Franc-Comtois, but also his capacity for hard work, his energy, and his ambition to rise in the world, to which his father's departure from the land to the city no doubt contributed. There were also his generosity towards those who sought his help and his ability to laugh at himself after a sharp burst of anger.[15]

The most important element of his character was his intellectual ability and quickness to learn. Perhaps because he remained for so long an only child—he was twelve when his sister was born—and received a good deal of personal attention from his parents and grandmother, he demonstrated great academic ability in his days as a student at the *collège* of Lure. There he won an impressive number of prizes during his last three years (1887-1890), particularly in languages, science, and history. In addition, in each of these three years, he won either the first or second award for scholarship.[16]

In the autumn of 1890, young Albert transferred to the *lycée* at Vesoul, the *chef-lieu* of the Haute-Saône Department. During his year there he earned numerous honors, including the first prize in history. Albert Troux has recorded that the young student

> one day amazed an inspector general who was passing through by the clarity and originality of a history recitation that his teacher had called upon him to give. The inspector not only encouraged him to pursue his studies, but even secured the extension and transfer of his scholarship to Paris.[17]

Mathiez's departure for Paris took him from the rural Haute-Saône to the great city. But by the time he entered the *lycée* of Sceaux in 1891, his character had already been formed. Thanks to the recollections of the historian Jules Isaac, then a young boarding student at Lakanal, we can visualize the young Mathiez as he had become and would remain for the next forty years. According to Isaac, Mathiez was "astonishingly large and square-shouldered, with a somewhat low-set head, a thin and prominent nose in a pallid face. His speech was cutting. He was . . . violently impulsive, hot-tempered, easily angered, rebellious and apt to express extreme opinions." At Sceaux, Mathiez became friendly with Albert Lévy, son of an Alsatian rabbi; Louis-Victor Bourrilly a hard-working Provençal; and a promising student

15 The character of the inhabitants of the province is discussed in Georges Gazier, *La Franche-Comté* (Paris, 1924), pp. 74-77. Cf. Jules Isaac, *Expériences de ma vie: Péguy* (Paris, 1960), p. 47.

16 Archives, Ecole Normale Supérieure (Paris). Personal file of Albert Mathiez (1893).

17 Albert Troux, *Un Grand Historien comtois, Albert Mathiez (1874-1932)* (Nancy, 1935), p. 10.

from Orléans, Charles Péguy. The four students got along well from the outset, and Péguy, "grave, wrought-up, thoughtful, but still a good and cheerful companion," tolerated the outbursts of violent temper by the young Franc-Comtois. If Mathiez was quick to anger, he was also quick to calm himself and to laugh with his friends over his rages.[18]

Already Mathiez's political outlook had begun to develop. According to Isaac, Mathiez and Péguy had evolved towards socialism, "that adolescent socialism with its still undefined contours and shape."[19] In 1892, report the Tharaud brothers in their biography of Péguy, Mathiez "took up a subscription to aid the striking coal miners of Carmaux. Péguy was the first to contribute and to hurl fire and flame against the company which was violating the strikers' rights."[20]

Mathiez was attracted to socialism for three reasons. First, he sprang from the peasant class which valued hard work, yet was unable to make a decent living from its labor. Mathiez sensed that the existing social and economic structure was unjust, and that social reform was necessary, reform that the older political parties could not or would not carry out.

But Mathiez was also an intellectual critic of society, a member of the intelligentsia which repudiated the materialism and selfishness of the wealthy and powerful. Here the element of moralism was strong. He felt a sense of righteousness that his generation would rise above the mistakes of the past and lead society to a brighter future. The new socialism that was growing would cleanse the evils of capitalism and impose a new social order in which the working class and its intellectual partisans would govern.

A third factor that contributed to this feeling was the emergence of a young generation which had not known the authoritarian Second Empire, the heroic days of the Franco-Prussian War, or the agonies of the Commune. In the year Mathiez was born, 1874, the troops of the German occupier at last withdrew from French soil, but the fate of the Third Republic still remained very much in doubt. The moral order of Broglie and MacMahon held sway and a monarchical restoration remained a possibility. By the time Mathiez entered his teens, the republic had been firmly established. It soon became the "debased ideal" that made Alphonse Aulard sigh, "How fair the Republic was, under the Empire."[21] After the May 16 crisis of 1877, and the triumph of the republicans, came the presidency of Jules Grévy, who was forced to resign because of his son-in-law's misdeeds, and the conservative republic of the Opportunists, many of whom were implicated in the Panama Scandal. Mathiez grew to manhood in a period when ministers

18 Isaac, *Expériences*, pp. 37-40.
19 Ibid., p. 49.
20 Jerome and Jean Tharaud, *Notre cher Péguy*, 2 vols. (Paris, 1926), I, 18.
21 Georges Belloni, *Aulard, Historien de la Révolution française* (Paris, 1949), pp. 94-95.

were more interested in seeking personal gain than in relieving the depressed social and economic condition of the working class.

The celebration in 1889 of the centennial of the Revolution, with its great international exposition, may well have awakened young men like Mathiez to the gulf that existed between the revolutionary rhetoric of the republicans in power and their meager accomplishments.

Finally, the growing strength of socialism at the polls, at the municipal level in 1892 and in the legislative elections of the following year, gave Mathiez and his friends the feeling that socialism was on the march. It was in 1892 that Jean Jaurès became a convert to the socialist cause, largely through the efforts of Lucien Herr, librarian of the Ecole Normale Supérieure.

When they themselves entered the Ecole Normale in the autumn of 1894, Mathiez and his friends from Lakanal, Péguy and Lévy, as well as Georges Weulersse, nephew of Georges Renard (who had been involved in the Paris Commune of 1871), lived together in a study room that soon acquired the name "Utopia." The four shared a socialism that was republican, anti-clerical, and idealistic. Péguy summed up their beliefs in a letter written to a friend in May, 1895, after he had formally joined the French Socialist Party. He spoke of an "ideal state of humanity":

> a state in which the least possible of necessary material human labor would be wasted, so as to give humanity the most leisure possible; an equal division of leisure among all men without exception, permitting them all to collaborate in the elevated human labor of thought or feeling, after their necessary material work. . . .
> Socialism has made very rapid progress. In large degree it is bringing together the best forces in the country. In opposition the governmental bourgeoisie is making alliances with all the forces of oppression, which call themselves conservative: the churches, banks, large-scale industry, big business, the army—in a word, all the powers.
> At this moment, and no doubt for a rather long time, I am following the march of the French socialists. . . . Lévy and Mathiez are doing the same. Of course the reasons that impel them to do so are shared by us all, but they also have other, personal, ones.[22]

According to the Tharaud brothers, the occupants of "Utopia" did not simply adhere to a "fierce socialist orthodoxy"; they also led a "crusade to convert [their] comrades to the socialist faith. They each took responsibility for a certain number of lectures in which they expressed the pure doctrine." The four probably found a sympathetic audience, for at least half of those who entered in 1894 became converts to socialism. Only a few years before, there were no socialists at the Ecole Normale.[23]

---

22 *Feuillets de l'amitié Charles Péguy*, 10 (March, 1950), 2-3.
23 Tharaud, *Notre cher Péguy*, I, 66, 84-85; Elie Halevy, *L'Ere des tyrannies: Etudes sur le socialisme et la guerre* (Paris, 1938),p. 216; cf. Robert J. Smith, "L'Atmosphère politique à l'Ecole Normale Supérieure à la fin du XIXe Siècle," *Revue d'histoire modern et contemporaine*, 22 (1973), 248-68.

But Mathiez's socialism remained essentially republican. Paul Mantoux has left us a description of his friend which makes this clear:

> He was or believed himself to be a socialist. What lived in him was the spirit of 1793. In the small group of extreme opinion to which he and Péguy (then a convinced socialist) belonged, his voice resounded like an echo of the revolutionary assemblies. We called him "The Citizen."[24]

Hubert Bourgin, another *normalien*, but one who later turned against socialism, expressed his doubts:

> Was he ever a socialist? He did not belong to our organizations in the Ecole Normale and the Latin Quarter, was not one of us, and never cooperated with Péguy any more than he did with us. . . . He seemed to have the temperament of a Jacobin. At least he had the appearance, the gestures, the words, and the allure of one.[25]

This socialism was strongly anti-clerical. If Mathiez's anti-clericalism was of long standing, its origins are uncertain. He certainly had religious training as a child, but as early as his days at the *collège* of Lure, he showed a certain lack of enthusiasm for professed religion. Though generally a good student, "at catechism the children of the bourgeoisie who were instructed by their mothers in prayer, sacred history, etc., were superior to him." Mathiez later boasted of his youthful impiety when he told his children that on the morning of his first communion he and a friend gorged themselves on cherries they had picked from a tree.[26]

At the Ecole Normale both Mathiez and Péguy belonged to the anti-clerical students who displayed contempt for their Catholic and clerical comrades. The two mocked their conservative teacher of philosophy, Ollé-Laprune, by singing the pious song "Oh, Sacred Heart of Jesus" before he arrived in class.[27]

A few years later, during the Dreyfus Affair, Mathiez became a member of the League of the Rights of Man, and while teaching at the *lycée* of Caen, vigorously supported the separation of Church and State. This, he argued, was a return to the tradition of the French Revolution.[28] After the World War, Mathiez sharply criticized the conservative Bloc National for not extending the Law of Separation to Alsace-Lorraine, for re-establishing diplomatic relations with the Vatican, and for instituting the national fête of Jeanne d'Arc.[29]

Yet Mathiez was no rabid anti-clerical who blamed all evils in France on Catholicism. As an historian he could compliment those clerics who produced sincere historical work on the Revolution and

24 Mantoux, "Albert Mathiez," p. 88.
25 Hubert Bourgin, *De Juarès à Léon Blum: L'Ecole Normale et la Politique* (Paris, 1938), p. 271.
26 Information given to the author by Mme Albert Lautman.
27 Félicien Challaye, *Péguy socialiste* (Paris, 1954), p. 40.
28 *Le Journal de Caen*, December 19-20, 1904.
29 Friguglietti, *Albert Mathiez*, p. 170.

denounce laymen like Pierre de la Gorce who let religious feelings color their historical judgments. It might also be noted that when Mathiez remarried in 1918, he took part in a religious ceremony held in the cathedral of St. Pierre in Besançon, and his wife would die in 1927, with the sacraments of the Church.[30]

Although a republican and anti-clerical, he was no Marxist. If Mathiez had become a socialist by the time he entered the Ecole Normale, he never accepted Marxism as an ideology. From the list of books he borrowed from the school library, we know that virtually everything he read dealt with history or geography. The sole exception was a biography of Blanqui written by Gustave Geffroy. Nor did Péguy and Lévy read Marxist texts. Only Georges Weulersse, whose uncle Georges Renard edited the *Revue socialiste*, is known to have done so. Anything Mathiez knew about Marxism he probably learned through Weulersse.[31]

Mathiez's interest in socialism was reinforced by the writings of Jaurès, whose *Histoire socialiste* appeared between 1901 and 1904. Having concentrated his attention almost exclusively on the political and religious history of the Revolution, Mathiez opened his eyes to an interpretation of the period far different from that of his mentor Aulard. He now began to realize the importance of historical materialism and the class struggle. By 1904 Mathiez could declare that "increasingly ... economic history appears to be the foundation of political history. Certainly we will be better placed to understand and to judge fairly the work of the Revolutionaries if we first measure with precision the terrible economic difficulties which they had to face."[32] Later that same year, Mathiez presented a talk on the social question during the Revolution in which he dealt with class conflict and the triumph of the bourgeoisie over both the established aristocracy and the emerging proletariat. But he referred only once to Marx, quoting him as saying that the Le Chapelier Law of 1791 was a "crime" against the working class.[33]

Two other factors contributed to his socialism: his bitter quarrel with Aulard and his distaste for the politics of the Third Republic. Mathiez's break with Aulard is well known but little understood. When the two scholars first met in 1900, their relationship seemed completely cordial. The older man directed his pupil's doctoral dissertation and promoted his publications, and the younger praised his teachers' scholarship and erudition. But differences in age—Aulard was born in 1849—in temperament—Aulard was a Voltaireian skeptic—and in

30 Information given to the author by Mme Albert Lautman.
31 Library records, Ecole Normal Supérieure (Paris, 1894-1897), cf. Eugene van Itter-
    beek, "Les Emprunts de Péguy à la bibliothèque de l'Ecole Normale," *Feuillets de
    l'amitié Charles Péguy*, 86 (August, 1961), 4-13.
32 *La Révolution française*, 46 (1904), p. 175.
33 *La Question sociale pendant la Révolution française* (Paris, 1905).

political outlook—Aulard was closely tied to the ruling Radical party—gradually led Mathiez to dislike his teacher, question his research, and even to doubt his intellectual integrity. His own extensive research and use of Aulard's documentary collections, particularly the *Actes du comité de salut public*, convinced him that they were not only inaccurate and incomplete, but largely the work of "scribes" to whom Aulard gave no credit, but for whose work he received a substantial subsidy from the government. In his eyes, Aulard was reduced to a "journalist" in the service of the Radical Republic, rewarded with honors and positions for his faithful support.

The more he grew to dislike Aulard as an historian, the more Mathiez saw in him a neo-Danton, who possessed all the failings of the corrupt, opportunistic orator of the Revolution. Aulard had facilitated this identification by the praise he heaped on Danton as a superb orator, sincere patriot, dedicated republican, and defender of the lay state. In 1889 he had succeeded in getting a statue of Danton erected on the Boulevard Saint-Germain, not far from the Sorbonne.[34]

In reaction, Mathiez turned for his own inspiration to Danton's rival, Robespierre, whom Aulard had condemned for his religious and political dictatorship, and for the "murder" of Danton. Though it is difficult to trace in detail, Mathiez's process of psychological identification with the Incorruptible was completed by 1907-1908, when he helped to found the Société des Etudes Robespierristes. He was further encouraged in his beliefs by the socialists Edmond Lockroy and Gustave Rouanet, who edited the *Revue socialiste* from 1898 to 1904.

In Robespierre Mathiez discerned a proponent of social action and democracy, a "modern" man rather than an outdated historical figure, the very type of leader who was needed in the Republic of Comrades. There seems little doubt that Mathiez was disappointed by the failure of the Chamber to produce the social and economic reforms expected once Church and State had been separated. While they did little to improve the lot of the worker, France's deputies increased their own salaries, engaged in political maneuvers, and protected those involved in such sordid financial deals as the illegal disposal of Church property.[35] When in 1911 Mathiez undertook to teach a course on parliamentary corruption during the Terror, he identified the dishonest politicians of the Third Republic with the *pourris* of the First: Fabre d'Eglantine, Basire, Chabot, and their leader Danton.[36]

Mathiez's socialism also took the form of anti-militarism. Like so many other young intellectuals of the day, he turned against the army,

34 Mathiez's relationship with Aulard is discussed in Friguglietti, *Albert Mathiez*, pp. 71-80.
35 "Y a-t-il une Renaissance religieuse en France?" *Grande Revue* (May, 1915), 419.
36 "Un Document sur la venalité de Danton," *Annales révolutionnaires*, 4 (1911), 526-30; "La Fortune de Danton," ibid., 5 (1912), 453-77. "Encore la fortune de Danton," ibid., 6 (1913), 345-60.

its regimentation, conservatism, and ties to the Church by the Dreyfus Affair. Writing to his friend Péguy in 1900 Mathiez could speak in the same breath of the "clerical, capitalist and militarist threat."[37] A few years later, as president of the Caen section of the League of the Rights of Man, he secured the passage of resolutions which called for the disarming of soldiers while off duty and the elimination of a separate officers' mess.[38] We have it on good authority that after the presidential election of 1913, Mathiez exclaimed "Poincaré means war!"[39] Finally, on the eve of the international conflict, in March, 1914, he and a hundred other intellectuals published a manifesto denouncing the "armed peace" which existed and called upon Frenchmen to renounce their hopes of regaining Alsace-Lorraine so that peace with Germany could be assured.[40]

The outbreak of the World War drastically changed Mathiez's political views, for the German invasion and the formation of the Union Sacrée government turned him into a Jacobin nationalist. In the opening months of the war, he denounced Germany and her people, and called for the annexation of the Left Bank of the Rhine. Within a short time, however, he ceased these strident demands and concentrated on explaining how the First Republic had triumphed over the powers of the Old Regime in 1793-1794. (Here he put his extensive knowledge of the Revolution to good use.) An ardent republican, Mathiez also began to complain bitterly about the arbitrary policies of the government, its abuse of secrecy and censorship, its subservience to the military, and its failure to adopt strong economic measures to control inflation and scarcity.[41]

The anti-German feeling which the war aroused in him further turned him against socialism. He repeatedly denounced Marxism as a "poison" spread from beyond the Rhine, as a false doctrine which had led French socialism astray from the path beginning with the Revolution and continuing through 1848 and 1871. Mathiez expressed contempt for Jules Guesde and his followers whose "foreign" ideology made them more concerned with materialism than with idealism and who repudiated the work of Robespierre.[42]

It was, therefore, not Marxist doctrine that led him to hail both the March and November 1917 revolutions in Russia. The first toppled the old regime of aristocracy and autocracy, while the second rid Russia of its "Girondin" government which had failed to solve the agrarian

37 J. Frigualietti, "Péguy et Albert Mathiez," *Feuillets de l'amitié Charles Péguy*, 181 (October, 1972), 17-18.
38 *Bulletin officiel de la ligue des Droits-de-l'Homme*, 6 (1906), 1689.
39 Information given to the author by Mme Albert Lautman.
40 Marcel Laurent, Philippe Norard, and Alexandre Merceau, *La Paix armée et le problème d'Alsace dans l'opinion des nouvelles générations françaises* (Paris, 1914).
41 On Mathiez's changing attitudes during the conflict, see James Frigualietti, "Albert Mathiez, an Historian at War," *French Historical Studies*, 7 (Fall 1972), 570-86.
42 "Socialisme français et socialisme prussien," *L'Heure*, January 3, 1917.

question or to prosecute the war effectively. To Mathiez, the Bolsheviks reincarnated the Montagnards of 1793, and he fully expected them to continue the struggle against Germany. Angered by the peace of Brest-Litovsk, he wrote nothing more about the Soviet government until 1920.[43]

By 1920 he had warmed to the new Russia, believing that he was witnessing the events of 1792-1794 re-enacted, with Lenin appearing as the new Robespierre. As Mathiez commented:

> Jacobinism, Bolshevism—these words sum up the desire for justice by an oppressed class which is freeing itself from its chains. The strength of Robespierre and Lenin results from their understanding of their troops, their ability to discipline, and satisfy, and inspire confidence in them. In spite of appearances, dictators do not base their power on an authority above the people, on torture and constraint. No! Their strength and prestige arise from public opinion.
>   Lenin is filled . . . with the examples and lessons of our great Jacobin Revolution. He has erected a statue to Robespierre. He knows what he owes to him.[44]

His identification of Soviet Russia with the Montagnard Republic, his disgust for the conservative Bloc National, as well as his contempt for the Left which had failed to prevent wartime concessions to the military and the Church, led him to ally himself with the Communist Party after the split within the Socialist Party in 1920.

The two years that Mathiez spent in the Communist Party were devoted to attacks on the reactionary government and its policies. He considered the Communists to be the only true revolutionary force in France, the vanguard of social and economic change, and the only group which had not compromised itself in the political game. Contributing regularly to the party newspapers *L'Humanité*, *L'Internationale*, and *Le Populaire de Bourgogne*, Mathiez used his acid pen and extensive historical knowledge to assail the regime, which he called "another name for imperialist and clerical capitalism." He singled out Premier Poincaré for special attack, labeling him "the man of the capitalist, imperialist and militarist reaction," "the war president who was also president of the monarchists."[45]

But if Mathiez greatly admired Lenin, defended the Soviet Union, and followed the party line, he remained at heart the same independent spirit who could not bear to be dominated or directed by others. By mid-1922 he grew uncomfortable with his role as a Communist. In an open letter to *Le Populaire de Bourgogne*, he declared:

> I cannot conceive of a dictatorship within the party. A dictatorship is permissible only in periods of catastrophe when its exercise is unavoida-

43 "Vive la Russie!" *Le Petit comtois*, March 17, 1917; "Heures graves en Russie," ibid., September 12, 1917; "La Chute de Kerenski," ibid., November 10, 1917.
44 "Lénine et Robespierre," *Floréal*, June 12, 1920, p. 429.
45 "M. Poincaré continue," *L'Internationale*, September 21, 1921; "Poincaré-le Véridique," *L'Humanité*, February 4, 1922.

ble. But it is madness to imagine that sacrifices can be secured from men through passive obedience. Commands ordered from on high and imposed without discussion are good only for slaves. Free men will always refuse to obey them. As much discipline as is necessary, but discipline freely given and understood. The French party cannot execute orders the inappropriateness of which is all too evident. France is not Russia![46]

By year's end he had left the party, incensed by the dictatorship which he felt the Third International exerted over it. "I've left *L'Humanité*," he wrote to a friend in December, "and I shall not return unless the party knows how to make itself respected in Moscow and brings its paid agents to heel."[47]

Mathiez soon reverted to the independent socialism he had followed before the World War. He became associated with the newly formed Union socialiste communiste formed at Dijon in 1923, which hoped to bridge the gap between the major parties of the Left, and later with the S. F. I. O. In 1926-1927 he contributed several articles to the *Nouvelle revue socialiste* of Jean Longuet. Elated by the victory of the Left in the elections of 1924, he soon had reason to attack the government anew when Poincaré returned to power two years later. He spoke of it as "a regime which has only the appearance of democracy," "this regime which calls itself democratic but which mocks universal suffrage."[48]

Partly in reaction to the nationalist policies of Poincaré, Mathiez reverted to his prewar pacifism during the 1920s. In 1926 he signed an *Appeal to Consciences* which denounced the war-guilt clauses of the Versailles peace treaty and called for their abrogation.[49] Five years later he joined the League of the Fighters for Peace, which Victor Méric had founded to warn against the terrible dangers of a new world war. (Méric was appalled by the idea that in another conflict, aircraft and poison gas would destroy civilian population centers, causing the loss of millions of innocent lives.) But in September, 1931, after returning from a speaking tour in Germany, Mathiez quit the organization. In Germany, he explained, the spirit of revenge was too strong for there to be a chance of reconciliation.[50]

This same pattern of acceptance followed by rejection is apparent in Mathiez's attitude towards Marxism during these same years. Before 1914 he had never been committed to Marx's doctrines. But in the 1920s, perhaps because of the conservatism of Poincaré's government,

46 "Opinions libres: Une Lettre," *Le Populaire de Bourgogne*, July 28, 1922.
47 Letter to Maurice Dommanget, dated December 1922, communicated to the author by M. Dommanget.
48 "Danton, l'histoire et la légende," *Annales historiques de la Révolution française*, 4 (1927), 461.
49 "Un appel aux consciences," *Evolution*, January 15, 1926, p. 39; reprinted in Victor Margueritte, *La Patrie humaine* (Paris, 1931), 276-81.
50 Victor Méric, "Des Traites," *Le Soir*, September 29, 1931; "Sur un Disparu," ibid., February 28, 1932.

perhaps because of contacts with Soviet scholars, Mathiez began to call himself a Marxist. He did so publicly before his classes at the Sorbonne: "As a good Marxist which I have the honor of being," he remarked one day during a lecture.[51] In a letter to a friend written in 1929, he stated that:

> The First Republic was struck down when it continually violated the principles of liberty and equality to which it appealed. But, in my view as a Marxist [*pour mois qui suis marxiste*], neither principles nor methods are the true factors in the survival or destruction of states; they are economic and social factors.[52]

His friendship with Soviet historians, notably Eugene Tarle, his praise for their work in the pages of his journal, the *Annales historiques de la Révolution française*, the translation of his own works into Russian, and his election to membership in the Russian Academy of Sciences in 1927, all indicate both his faith in Marxist historical writing and his own acceptability to Soviet scholarship.[53]

But the sudden arrest of Tarle in 1930 after his return from a speaking engagement in France and the subsequent attacks made against him by Soviet scholars angered Mathiez. The first public indication of his changing attitude towards Marxism and the Soviet Union came when he published a lengthy note in the *Annales historiques de la Révolution française* that autumn. In it Mathiez spoke contemptuously of the methodology of Soviet historians as

> an *a priori* dogma, . . . a certain Marxism understood and practiced like a catechism. . . . In this country, history has too often ceased to be independent and docilely submits to the all-powerful pressure of politics which imposes its ideas, its pre-occupations, its passwords, and even its conclusions.[54]

These sharp comments drew a lengthy reply from eight Soviet historians who, after praising Mathiez's work, declared that whether he wished it or not, he was participating in the "fierce persecutions to which the [Workers' State] is subjected by the enemies of the emancipation of the working class, by those who want to keep humanity under the yoke of capitalism." "You thus become," they concluded, "one of the members of the united front of all the defenders of the capitalist order against the workers' state."[55]

51 Information given to the author by M. March Bouloiseau.
52 Letter to Alfred Rufer, dated March 9, 1929, communicated to the author by M. J. R. Suratteau.
53 "Les Travaux russes sur l'histoire de la Révolution française," *Annales historiques de la Révolution française*, 4 (1927), 589-92. For the Russian translations of Mathiez's works see ibid., 3 (1926), 596; 5 (1928), 494, 599; 6 (1929), 107. On Mathiez's election to the Russian Academy of Sciences, see ibid., 5 (1928), 192.
54 "Le Neuf Thermidor dans la nouvelle littérature historique," *Annales historiques de la Révolution française*, 6 (1930), 401.
55 "Choses de Russie sovietique," ibid., 8 (1931), 150-51.

Greatly irritated, Mathiez replied with a vehement denunciation of the eight historians for allowing their colleague Tarle to be imprisoned unjustly. He attacked their views of Marxism as a valid instrument of historical science, declaring that Marx and Engels seemed "often exceptionally foggy and I need clarity." He observed that their historical writing served to glorify Soviet communism, commenting bitterly that "Stalin is God and you are his prophets. You are only tools in the hands of the government. You mask your surrender with the name of Marxism."[56] Mathiez completed his break with Marxist theory in 1931 when he wrote that he had "always considered Marxism as a fertile historical synthesis but only as an hypothesis."[57]

His retreat from Marxism because of Stalin's authoritarian rule represented a return to his old intellectual independence, his inability to accept domination by anyone or any doctrine not of his own making. Writing to the American historian, Louis Gottschalk, in 1930, Mathiez declared:

> I have a horror of abstract constructions. . . . It would be wrong to catalogue me in some pigeonhole, in a handbook. I love life and enjoy envisaging its complexity, both in the general and in the particular.[58]

Republican, anti-clerical, Dreyfusard, socialist, anti-militarist, Communist, and Marxist—Mathiez was, at one time or another, all of these. But it was to Robespierrism that he remained most consistently faithful. From the time of the foundation of the Société des Etudes Robespierristes in 1907 until his untimely death in 1932, he fought vigorously to rehabilitate the memory of the Incorruptible. In a constant stream of writings and speeches, Mathiez sought to strip away the legends and calumnies which had covered his true reputation and to show Robespierre as the incarnation of the "most noble, most generous, and most sincere aspect of Revolutionary France."[59]

Mathiez's idealization, even idolization, of Robespierre stems not simply from his desire to create a model for citizens of the Third Republic. He was also satisfying some deep-seated psychological need to destroy the reputation of Danton, and that of Danton's defender and his own rival, Aulard. This explains why Mathiez could find no fault with his hero, except perhaps that of being "too mild."[60]

Today this devotion to Robespierre seems excessive, for historians have gone beyond Mathiez's work of rehabilitation to trace a more human and less idealized portrait. It is now fair to say that Danton, despite his venality, contributed to the defense of the Republic in 1792-1793.

56 Ibid., 152-54.
57 *Monde*, July 25, 1931, p. 14.
58 "Une Lettre d'Albert Mathiez," *Annales historiques de la Révolution française*, 9 (1932), 219.
59 *Robespierre terroriste* (Paris, 1921), p. 188.
60 Ibid., p. 24.

But if some of his historical judgments have been superseded, in reading Mathiez's works we can still feel the excitement and vigor he brought to the study of the Revolution. His lively style stemmed directly from the enthusiasm he had for the period and his keen awareness of the individuals who took part in it. To Mathiez the Revolution was no distant historical event, but rather one that was still current. Was it merely by chance that he chose to live on the Rue de la Convention at Besançon, Boulevard Carnot at Dijon, and Rue Vergniaud at Paris, or that he took the number 93 tram each day on his way to classes at the Sorbonne?

His inability to ease up in his unrelenting labors on behalf of the Revolution finally killed him when he was at the peak of his career. The enthusiasm and passion which he displayed in his work were natural to him, and he gloried in them. Writing in 1924 he justified his work in a kind of historical testament:

> It is because I believe in the social virtue of history and because I am convinced that it offers lessons for statesmen and citizens that I cannot undertake its study without feeling a sense of responsibility.
> Humanity will always move blindly toward the future if it is unable to profit from the experience of the past. History is a mirror, and if the mirror distorts the image, it misleads the guide.
> This lofty idea which I have of the function of history perhaps explains why I have been criticized for my passion, of which I am proud. It is enough if I have not been accused of poor, petty passions which reveal political fanaticism, a spirit of cliquishness, false friendship or partisanship, the desire for honors and positions. In sum, the only thing which annoys my discreet critics is my independence.[61]

Without this passion, this fierce spirit of independence born of his Franc-Comtois and peasant origins, Mathiez would never have risen as far as he did, or made the contribution to historical understanding that he made. True, when this passion was expressed in angry denunciations of opponents for what he considered their weak scholarship or unsound political opinions, it was often excessive. Too frequently he quarrelled and broke with associates who had been his good friends, joined and then left movements because he felt his personal integrity threatened. His students were the most immediate beneficiaries (and sometimes victims) of his enthusiasm. In the words of one of them, Robert Schnerb, "Ah! How he could grasp the Revolutionaries of 1789 and 1793, and in a voice that alternated between enthusiasm and derision, bring them to life. It was an astonishing performance, . . . one that never left us indifferent."[62] Or as his friend and former student, Edmond Campagnac, declared: "He was one of those who feel that history should be passionate in order to be true."[63]

61 *Autour de Robespierre* (Paris, 1925), p. 8.
62 Robert Schnerb, "Souvenirs sur l'enseignement d'Albert Mathiez à la faculté des lettres de Dijon," *Annales historiques de la Révolution française*, 9 (1932), 254.
63 Edmond Campagnac, "L'Historien Albert Mathiez," *L'Ecole et la vie*, March 12, 1932, p. 399.

Almost a half century after Mathiez's death, those who did not know him personally can still experience in his writings the passion of which he was so proud. His books and articles continue to exert a hold on readers by their clear, sharp prose, which lends excitement to his ideas and force to his arguments. He possessed the rare ability to make the most familiar episodes of the Revolution seem fresh but by using the authority of the scholar rather than the romantic flourishes of the novelist. In each page we can still hear his powerful voice vibrating like that of an orator of the Convention, just as Paul Mantoux heard him in the corridors of the Ecole Normale. Even today, Albert Mathiez remains "The Citizen" whose energy was devoted to the defense of the Revolution and whose life was given in its service. He was, in the words of one who mourned his passing, "the ardent historian of an ardent history."[64]

64 "Adieu à Albert Mathiez," *Annales historiques de la Révolution française*, 9 (1932), 279.

Appendix: Publications by John Hall Stewart*

A. Books

1942   *France, 1715-1815: A Guide to Materials in Cleveland* (Cleveland, Ohio: Western Reserve University Press, 1942). Edition limited to 501 copies; pp. xxxiii, 522.

1951   *A Documentary Survey of the French Revolution* (New York: Macmillan, 1951; reprinted several times); pp. xxviii, 818.

1964   *The French Revolution from 1793 to 1799*, translation (in collaboration with James Friguglietti) of second part of Georges Lefebvre's *La Révolution française* (London: Routledge & Kegan Paul; and New York: Columbia University Press, 1964); pp. xiv, 430.

1967   *The French Revolution: Some Trends in Historical Writings, 1945-1965* (Washington, D.C.: American Historical Association, 1967); pp. vi, 37. No. 67 in Pamphlets Published by the Service Center for Teachers of History.

1968   *The Restoration Era in France: 1814-1830* (Princeton, N.J.: D. Van Nostrand Company, Inc., 1968); pp. 223. No. 98 in Anvil Series, ed. by Louis L. Snyder.

B. Portions of Books

1954   "The French Revolution and Napoleon," being chapter 10 (pp. 370-411) in *Great Problems in European Civilization*, ed. by Kenneth M. Setton and Henry R. Winkler (New York: Prentice-Hall, 1954; 2nd ed., 1966).

1958   "Thoughts and Afterthoughts," being chapter 11 (pp. 156-73) of *Carl Becker's Heavenly City Revisited*, ed. by Raymond O. Rockwood, with introduction by George H. Sabine (Ithaca, N.Y.: Cornell University Press, 1958).

1961   Sections on the French Revolution (pp. 473-75) and biographies of leading figures of the Revolution (pp. 491-92) in *The American Historical Association's Guide to Historical Literature*, George Frederick Howe, Chairman of the Board of Editors (New York: Macmillan, 1961).

* Exclusive of book reviews.

1967   "Danton and Robespierre," being chapter 13 (pp. 388-420) of
       vol. 1 of *Interpreting European History*, ed. by Brison D. Gooch, 2
       vols. (Homewood, Ill.: The Dorsey Press, 1967).

C. Articles

1928   "Rabaut-Pommier and the Discovery of Vaccine," *American
       Medicine*, New Series, vol. 23, no. 3 (March 1928), 195-99.
1930   "Why are Canadian Teachers in United States Universities?"
       Maclean's Magazine, Toronto, Canada, October 15, 1930.
1932   "The Ottawa Conference—What Has That to do with Cleve-
       land?" (co-author) *Cleveland Mid-Week Review*, November 9 and
       16, 1932.
1933   "A Concentrated Major in History and Literature" (with Win-
       field H. Rogers), *English Journal*, College Edition (October
       1933), 674-76.
1935   "If I Were a Canadian Minister of Education," *Saturday Night*,
       Toronto, Canada (Weekly), June 15, 1935.
1936   Dictatorship by the Ballot," *Saturday Night*, Toronto, Canada
       (Weekly), August 29, 1936.
       "Southern New Year," *Saturday Night,* Toronto, Canada
       (Weekly), December 26, 1936.
1950   "I Have Seen Malahide Castle," *St. Thomas Times-Journal*, St.
       Thomas, Ontario, March 18, 1950.
       "Historians and Their Helpers," *Ohio State Archaeological and
       Historical Quarterly* (April 1950), 154-64.
       "First Impressions of Dublin," *The Plain Dealer*, Cleveland,
       Ohio, April 22, 1950.
       "An American Visitor at the Bolton Brass Band Contest," *British
       Bandsman* (Weekly), London, England, May 20 and 27 and June
       3, 1950.
1951   "The British Brass Band," *Music Educators Journal* (April-May,
       1951), 30-32, 51-55.
       "Some Impressions of Dublin," *Alumnae Folio*, Flora Stone
       Mather college of Western Reserve University (May 1951).
       "The Norton Napoleon Collection," *Journal of Modern History*
       (June 1951), 158-62.
       "The Imprisonment of Napoleon: A Legal Opinion by Lord
       Eldon," *American Journal of International Law* (July 1951), 571-
       77.
1954   "The Fall of the Bastille on the Dublin Stage," *Journal of the
       Royal Society of Antiquaries of Ireland*, Part 1 (1954), 143-60.
1957   Group of articles on "Canada" in *American Peoples Encyclopedia*,
       20 vols. (Chicago, 1957ff.). Through oversight, author's name
       does not appear in list of contributors.

"The Era of the French Revolution: Opportunities for Research and Writing," *Journal of Modern History* (June 1957), 85-98. (Editing of three papers and of remarks of two commentators presented in a session at the meeting of the American Historical Association in 1955.)

1961 "The French Revolution on the Dublin Stage, 1790-1794," *Journal of the Royal Society of Antiquaries of Ireland,* Part 2 (1961), 183-92.

1962 "Poetry on the French Revolution in the Irish Press," *The Historian*, vol. 24, no. 2 (February 1962), 172-91.

"Burke's Reflections and the Irish Press," *French Historical Studies*, vol. 2, no. 3 (Spring 1962), 376-90.

"The Irish Press during the French Revolution," *Journalism Quarterly* (Autumn 1962), 507-18.

1972 "Beatrice Fry Hyslop: A Tribute," *French Historical Studies*, vol. 7, no. 4 (Fall 1972), 473-78.

Index